Donna Mathus

SELECTED POEMS
OF
EMILY DICKINSON

(handwritten annotations in right margin:)

p 15 (22)
22 (39)
31 (59)
32 (60)
37 (72)

? 38 (73)
/ 41 (79)
49 (98)
* 55 (111.
? 55 (112
58 (115
84 (30)
99 (57)
? 100 (60)
116 (84)

146 (25
151 (34
166 (8
167 (10

SELECTED POEMS

of

Emily Dickinson

with an introduction by CONRAD AIKEN

THE
MODERN LIBRARY
NEW YORK

The poems of this volume are selected from Poems, First, Second, and Third Series, published in 1890, 1891, and 1896, and here reprinted by permission of Little, Brown & Company.

Random House IS THE PUBLISHER OF

THE MODERN LIBRARY

BENNETT A. CERF · DONALD S. KLOPFER · ROBERT K. HAAS

Manufactured in the United States of America

By H. Wolff

CONTENTS

INTRODUCTION

ЕMILY DICKINSON was born in Amherst, Massachusetts, on De-
cember 10, 1830. She died there, after a life perfectly devoid of
outward event, in 1886. She was thus an exact contemporary of
Christina Rossetti, who was born five days earlier than she, and
outlived her by eight years. Of her life we know little. Her father,
Edward Dickinson, was a lawyer, and the Treasurer of Amherst
College; and it is clear that what social or intellectual life was in
that bleak era available, was available for her. That she did not
choose to avail herself of it, except in very slight degree, is also
clear; and that this choice, which was gradually to make of her
life an almost inviolable solitude, was made early, is evident from
her Letters. In a letter dated 1853, when she was twenty-three
years old, she remarked, "I do not go from home." By the time
she was thirty, the habit of sequestration had become distinct, a
subject on which she was explicit and emphatic in her letters to
T. W. Higginson—essayist and contributor to the *Atlantic*

Monthly at that time. She made it clear that if there was to be any question of a meeting between them, he would have to come to Amherst—she would not go to Boston. Higginson, as a matter of fact, saw her twice, and his record of the encounter is practically the only record we have of her from any "literary" personage of her lifetime. Even this is meager—Higginson saw her superficially, as was inevitable. Brave soldier, courtly gentleman, gifted amateur of letters, he was too much of the old school not to be a little puzzled by her poetry; and if he was fine enough to guess the fineness, he was not quite fine enough wholly to understand it. The brief correspondence between these two is an extraordinary document of unconscious irony—the urbanely academic essayist reproaching his wayward pupil for her literary insubordination, her false quantities, and reckless liberties with rhyme; the wayward pupil replying with a humility, beautiful and pathetic, but remaining singularly, with unmalleable obstinacy, herself. "I saw her," wrote Higginson, "but twice, face to face, and brought away the impression of something as unique and remote as Undine or Mignon or Thekla." When, thirty years after the acquaintance had begun, and four after Emily Dickinson's death, he was asked for assistance and advice in making a selection from her poetry, practically none of which had been published during her lifetime, his scruples were less severe, and he spoke of her with generosity and insight. "After all," he then wrote, "when a thought takes one's breath away, a lesson on grammar seems an impertinence." Again, "In many cases these verses will seem to the reader like poetry torn up by the roots." And again, "a quality more suggestive of the poetry of Blake than of anything to be elsewhere found—flashes of wholly original and profound insight into nature and life."

Thus began and ended Emily Dickinson's only important connection with the literary life of her time. She knew, it is true, Helen Hunt Jackson, a poetess, for whose anthology, *A Masque of Poets*, she gave the poem "Success," one of the few poems she allowed publication during her life. And she knew the Bowles family, owners and editors of the *Springfield Republican*, at that time the *Manchester Guardian* of New England—which, as she put it mischievously, was one of "such papers . . . as have nothing carnal in them." But these she seldom saw; and aside from these she had few intimates outside of her family; the circle of her world grew steadily smaller. This is a point of cardinal importance, but unfortunately no light has been thrown upon it. It is apparent that Miss Dickinson became a hermit by deliberate and conscious choice. "A recluse," wrote Higginson, "by temperament and habit, literally spending years without setting her foot beyond the doorstep, and many more years during which her walks were strictly limited to her father's grounds, she habitually concealed her mind, like her person, from all but a very few friends; and it was with great difficulty that she was persuaded to print, during her lifetime, three or four poems." One of the co-editors of Poems: Second Series assures us that this voluntary hermitage was not due to any "love-disappointment," and that she was "not an invalid." "She had tried society and the world, and had found them lacking." But this, of course, tells us nothing. Her Letters show us convincingly that her girlhood was a normally "social" one—she was active, high-spirited, and endowed with a considerable gift for extravagant humor. As a young woman she had, so Mrs. Bianchi, a niece, informed us in the preface to *The Single Hound*, several "love-affairs," but there is no evidence that any of them was serious, and we have no right, without other testimony, to assume here any ground for the singular psychological change that came over her. The only other clue we have, of any sort, is the hint from one of her girlhood friends, that, perhaps, *"she was longing for poetic sympathy."* Perhaps! But this, too, tells us very little. Anecdotes relating to her mischievousness, her wit, her waywardness, are not enough. It is amusing, if horrifying, to know that once, being anxious to dispose of some kittens, she put them on a shovel, carried them into the cellar, and dropped them into the nearest jar—which, subsequently, on the occasion of the visit of a distinguished judge, turned out to have been the pickle-jar. We like to know, too, that even when her solitude was most remote she was in the habit of lowering from her window, by a string, small baskets of fruit or confectionery for children. But there are other things we should like to know much more.

There seems now, however, little likelihood of our ever learning anything more; and if we seek for the causes of the psychic injury which so sharply turned her in upon herself, we can only speculate. Her letters, in this regard, give little light, only showing us again and again that the injury was deep. Of the fact that she suffered acutely from intellectual drought, there is evidence enough. One sees her vividly here—but one sees her, as it were, perpetually in retreat; always discovering anew, with dismay, the intellectual limitations of her correspondents; she is discreet, pathetic, baffled, a little humbled, and draws in her horns; takes sometimes a perverse pleasure in indulging more than ever, on the occasion of such a disappointment, in her love of a cryptic style—a delicate bombardment of parable and whim which she perfectly knows will stagger; and then again retreats to the safe ground of the superficial. It is perhaps for this reason that the letters give us so remarkably little information about her literary interests. The meagerness of literary allusion is astounding. The Brontës and the Brownings are referred to—she thought Alexander Smith "not very coherent"—Joaquin Miller she "could not care about." Of her own work she speaks only in the brief unsatisfactory correspondence with Higginson. To him she wrote in 1863, "I wrote no verse, but one or two, until this winter." Otherwise, no scrap of her own literary history: she appears to have existed in a vacuum. Of the literary events, tremendous for America, which were taking place during her most impressionable years, there is hardly a mention. Emerson was at the height of his career, and living only sixty miles away: his poems came out when she was seventeen. When she was twenty, Hawthorne published *The Scarlet Letter*, and *The House of Seven Gables* the year after. The same year, 1851, brought out Melville's *Moby Dick*. The death of Poe took place in 1849—in 1850 was published the first collected edition of his poems. When she was twenty-four, Thoreau's *Walden* appeared; when she was twenty-five, *Leaves of Grass*. One can say with justice that she came to full "consciousness" at the very moment when American literature came to flower. That she knew this, there cannot be any question; nor that she was stimulated and influenced by it. One must assume that she found in her immediate environment no one of her own stature, with whom she could admit or discuss such things; that she lacked the energy or effrontery to voyage out into the unknown in search of such companionship; and that lacking this courage, and wanting this help, she became easily a prey to the then current Emersonian doctrine of mystical individualism. In this connection it is permissible to suggest that her extreme self-seclusion and secrecy was both a protest and a display—a kind of vanity masquerading as modesty. She became increasingly precious, of her person as of her thought. Vanity is in her letters—at the last an unhealthy vanity. She believes that anything she says, however brief, will be of importance; however cryptic, will be deciphered. She enjoys being something of a mystery, and she sometimes deliberately and awkwardly exaggerates it. Even in notes of condolence—for which she had a morbid passion—she is vain enough to indulge in sententiousness: as when she wrote, to a friend whose father had died on her wedding-day, "Few daughters have the immortality of a father for a bridal gift."

When we come to Emily Dickinson's poetry, we find the Emersonian individualism clear enough, but perfectly Miss Dickinson's. Henry James observed of Emerson:

The doctrine of the supremacy of the individual to himself, of his originality and, as regards his own character, *unique* quality, must have had a great charm for people living in a society in which introspection, thanks to the want of other entertainment, played almost the part of a social resource. . . . There was . . . much relish for the utterances of a writer who would help one to take a picturesque view of one's internal possibilities, and to find in the landscape of the soul all sorts of fine sunrise and moonlight effects."

This sums up admirably the social "case" of Miss Dickinson— it gives us a shrewd picture of the causes of her singular introversion, and it suggests that we are perhaps justified in considering her the most perfect flower of New England Transcendentalism. In her mode of life she carried the doctrine of self-sufficient individualism farther than Thoreau carried it, or the naïve zealots of Brook Farm. In her poetry she carried it, with its complement of passionate moral mysticism, farther than Emerson: which is to say that as a poet she had more genius than he. Like Emerson, whose essays must greatly have influenced her, and whose poetry, especially his gnomic poems, only a little less, she was from the outset, and remained all her life, a singular mixture of Puritan and free thinker. The problems of good and evil, of life and death, obsessed her; the nature and destiny of the human soul; and Emerson's theory of compensation. Toward God, as one of her earliest critics is reported to have said, "she exhibited an Emersonian self-possession." Indeed, she did not, and could not, accept the Puritan God at all. She was frankly irreverent, on occasion, a fact which seems to have made her editors a little uneasy—one hopes that it has not resulted in the suppression of any of her work. What she was irreverent to, of course, was the Puritan conception of God, the Puritan attitude toward Him. In "Drowning" she observes:

> The Maker's cordial visage,
> However good to see,
> Is shunned, we must admit it,
> Like an adversity.

In one poem she refers to God as "a noted clergyman" and on another occasion she salutes Him as "Burglar, banker, father"—

a flippancy which might have annoyed even the most advanced of her contemporaries. But perhaps her perfect metaphysical detachment is most precisely and unabashedly stated in the famous mock-prayer (in "The Single Hound"), in which, addressing God, she quite impertinently apologizes to Him for His own "duplicity."

This, it must be repeated, is Emily Dickinson's opinion of the traditional and anthropomorphic "God," who was still, in her day, a portentous Victorian gentleman. Her real reverence, the reverence that made her a mystic poet of the finest sort, was reserved for Nature, which seemed to her a more manifest and more beautiful evidence of Divine Will than creeds and churches. This she saw, observed, loved, with a burning simplicity and passion which nevertheless did not exclude her very agile sense of humor. Her Nature poems, however, are not the most secretly revelatory or dramatically compulsive of her poems, nor, on the whole, the best. They are often of extraordinary delicacy—nearly always give us, with deft brevity, the exact in terms of the quaint. But, also, they are often superficial, a mere affectionate playing with the smaller things that give her delight; and to see her at her best and most characteristic and most profound, one must turn to the remarkable range of metaphysical speculation and ironic introspection which is displayed in those sections of her posthumous books which her editors have captioned Life, and Time and Eternity. In the former sections are the greater number of her set "meditations" on the nature of things. For some critics they will always appear too bare, bleak, and fragmentary. They have no trappings, only here and there a shred of purple. It is as if Miss Dickinson, who in one of her letters uttered her contempt for the "obtrusive body," had wanted to make them, as nearly as possible, disembodied thought. The thought is there, at all events, hard, bright, and clear; and her symbols, her metaphors, of which she could be prodigal, have an analogous clarity and translucency. What is also there is a downright homeliness which is a perpetual surprise and delight. Emerson's gnomic style she tunes up to the epigrammatic—the epigrammatic she often carries to the point of the cryptic; she becomes what one might call an epigrammatic symbolist.

> "Lay this laurel on the one
> Too intrinsic for renown.
> Laurel! veil your deathless tree,—
> Him you chasten, that is he!"

This, from Poems: Second Series, verges perilously on the riddle. And it often happens that her passionate devotion to concise statement in terms of metaphor left for her readers a small rich emblem of which the colors tease, the thought entices, but the meaning escapes. Against this, however, should be set her capacity, when occasion came, for a granite simplicity, any parallel to which one must seek in the seventeenth century. This, for example, called "Parting."

> "My life closed twice before its close;
> It yet remains to see
> If Immortality unveil
> A third event to me,
>
> So huge, so hopeless to conceive,
> As these that twice befell.
> Parting is all we know of heaven
> And all we need of hell."

Or this, from Poems: First Series:

> "I died for beauty, but was scarce
> Adjusted in the tomb,
> When one who died for truth was lain
> In an adjoining room.
>
> He questioned softly why I failed?
> 'For beauty,' I replied.

'And I for truth,—the two are one;
We brethren are,' he said.

And so, as kinsmen met at night,
We talked between the rooms,
Until the moss had reached our lips,
And covered up our names."

Both these poems, it will be noted, deal with death; and it must be observed that the number of poems by Miss Dickinson on this subject is one of the most remarkable things about her. Death, and the problem of life after death, obsessed her. She seems to have thought of it constantly—she died all her life, she probed death daily. "That bareheaded life under grass worries one like a wasp," she wrote. Ultimately, the obsession became morbid, and her eagerness for details, after the death of a friend—the hungry desire to know *how* she died—became almost vulture-like. But the preoccupation, with its horrible uncertainties—its doubts about immortality, its hatred of the flesh, and its many reversals of both positions—gave us her sharpest work. The theme was inexhaustible for her. If her poetry seldom became "lyrical," seldom departed from the colorless sobriety of its bare iambics and toneless assonance, it did so most of all when the subject was death. Death profoundly and cruelly invited her. It was most of all when she tried "to touch the smile," and dipped her "fingers in the frost," that she took full possession of her genius.

Her genius was, it remains to say, as erratic as it was brilliant. Her disregard for accepted forms or for regularities was incorrigible. Grammar, rhyme, meter—anything went by the board if it stood in the way of thought or freedom of utterance. Sometimes this arrogance was justified; sometimes not. She did not care in the least for variety of effect—of her six hundred-odd poems practically all are in octosyllabic quatrains or couplets, sometimes with rhyme, sometimes with assonance, sometimes with neither. Everywhere, when one first comes to these poems, one seems to see nothing but a colorless dry monotony. How deceptive a monotony, concealing what reserves of depth and splendor; what subtleties of mood and tone! Once adjust oneself to the spinsterly angularity of the mode, its lack of eloquence or rhetorical speed, its naïve and often prosaic directness, one discovers felicities of thought and phrase on every page. The magic is terse and sure. And ultimately one simply sighs at Miss Dickinson's singular perversity, her lapses and tyrannies, and accepts them as an inevitable part of the strange and original genius she was. The lapses and tyrannies become a positive charm—one even suspects they were deliberate. They satisfied her—therefore they satisfy us. This marks, of course, our complete surrender to her highly individual gift, and to the singular sharp beauty, present everywhere, of her personality. The two things cannot be separated; and together, one must suppose, they suffice to put her among the finest poets in the language.

Conrad Aiken

PART ONE

LIFE

This is my letter to the world,
    That never wrote to me, —
The simple news that Nature told,
    With tender majesty.

Her message is committed
    To hands I cannot see;
For love of her, sweet countrymen,
    Judge tenderly of me!

Success is counted sweetest
By those who ne'er succeed.
To comprehend a nectar
Requires sorest need.

Not one of all the purple host
Who took the flag to-day
Can tell the definition,
So clear, of victory,

As he, defeated, dying,
On whose forbidden ear
The distant strains of triumph
Break, agonized and clear.

Our share of night to bear,
Our share of morning,
Our blank in bliss to fill,
Our blank in scorning.

Here a star, and there a star,
Some lose their way.
Here a mist, and there a mist,
Afterwards—day!

Soul, wilt thou toss again?
By just such a hazard
Hundreds have lost, indeed,
But tens have won an all.

Angels' breathless ballot
Lingers to record thee;
Imps in eager caucus
Raffle for my soul.

4

'Tis so much joy! 'Tis so much joy!
If I should fail, what poverty!
And yet, as poor as I
Have ventured all upon a throw;
Have gained! Yes! Hesitated so
This side the victory!

Life is but life, and death but death!
Bliss is but bliss, and breath but breath!
And if, indeed, I fail,
At least to know the worst is sweet.
Defeat means nothing but defeat,
No drearier can prevail!

And if I gain,—oh, gun at sea,
Oh, bells that in the steeples be,
At first repeat it slow!
For heaven is a different thing
Conjectured, and waked sudden in,
And might o'erwhelm me so!

5

GLEE! the great storm is over!
Four have recovered the land;
Forty gone down together
Into the boiling sand.

[4]

Ring, for the scant salvation!
Toll, for the bonnie souls,—
Neighbor and friend and bridegroom,
Spinning upon the shoals!

How they will tell the shipwreck
When winter shakes the door,
Till the children ask, "But the forty?
Did they come back no more?"

Then a silence suffuses the story,
And a softness the teller's eye;
And the children no further question,
And only the waves reply.

6

IF I can stop one heart from breaking,
I shall not live in vain;
If I can ease one life the aching,
Or cool one pain,
Or help one fainting robin
Unto his nest again,
I shall not live in vain.

7

WITHIN my reach!
I could have touched!
I might have chanced that way!
Soft sauntered through the village,
Sauntered as soft away!
So unsuspected violets

[5]

Within the fields lie low,
Too late for striving fingers
That passed, an hour ago.

8

A WOUNDED deer leaps highest,
I've heard the hunter tell;
'Tis but the ecstasy of death,
And then the brake is still.

The smitten rock that gushes,
The trampled steel that springs:
A cheek is always redder
Just where the hectic stings!

Mirth is the mail of anguish,
In which it caution arm,
Lest anybody spy the blood
And "You're hurt" exclaim!

9

*T*HE heart asks pleasure first,
And then, excuse from pain;
And then, those little anodynes
That deaden suffering;

And then, to go to sleep;
And then, if it should be
The will of its Inquisitor,
The liberty to die.

A PRECIOUS, mouldering pleasure 'tis
To meet an antique book,
In just the dress his century wore;
A privilege, I think,

His venerable hand to take,
And warming in our own,
A passage back, or two, to make
To times when he was young.

His quaint opinions to inspect,
His knowledge to unfold
On what concerns our mutual mind,
The literature of old;

What interested scholars most,
What competitions ran
When Plato was a certainty,
And Sophocles a man;

When Sappho was a living girl,
And Beatrice wore
The gown that Dante deified.
Facts, centuries before,

He traverses familiar,
As one should come to town
And tell you all your dreams were true:
He lived where dreams were born.

His presence is enchantment,
You beg him not to go;

Old volumes shake their vellum heads
And tantalize, just so.

11

Much madness is divinest sense
To a discerning eye;
Much sense the starkest madness.
'Tis the majority
In this, as all, prevails.
Assent, and you are sane;
Demur,—you're straightway dangerous,
And handled with a chain.

12

I asked no other thing,
No other was denied.
I offered Being for it;
The mighty merchant smiled.

Brazil? He twirled a button.
Without a glance my way:
"But, madam, is there nothing else
That we can show to-day?"

13

The soul selects her own society,
Then shuts the door;
On her divine majority
Obtrude no more.

Unmoved, she notes the chariot's pausing
At her low gate;
Unmoved, an emperor is kneeling
Upon her mat.

I've known her from an ample nation
Choose one;
Then close the valves of her attention
Like stone.

14

SOME things that fly there be,—
Birds, hours, the bumble-bee:
Of these no elegy.

Some things that stay there be,—
Grief, hills, eternity:
Nor this behooveth me.

There are, that resting, rise.
Can I expound the skies?
How still the riddle lies!

15

I KNOW some lonely houses off the road
A robber'd like the look of,—
Wooden barred,
And windows hanging low,
Inviting to
A portico,

[9]

Where two could creep:
One hand the tools,
The other peep
To make sure all's asleep.
Old-fashioned eyes,
Not easy to surprise!

How orderly the kitchen'd look by night,
With just a clock,—
But they could gag the tick,
And mice won't bark;
And so the walls don't tell,
None will.

A pair of spectacles ajar just stir—
An almanac's aware.
Was it the mat winked,
Or a nervous star?
The moon slides down the stair
To see who's there.

There's plunder,—where?
Tankard, or spoon,
Earring, or stone,
A watch, some ancient brooch
To match the grandmamma,
Staid sleeping there.

Day rattles, too,
Stealth's slow;
The sun has got as far
As the third sycamore.

Screams chanticleer,
"Who's there?"

And echoes, trains away,
Sneer—"Where?"
While the old couple, just astir,
Think that the sunrise left the door ajar!

16

To fight aloud is very brave,
But gallanter, I know,
Who charge within the bosom,
The cavalry of woe.

Who win, and nations do not see,
Who fall, and none observe,
Whose dying eyes no country
Regards with patriot love.

We trust, in plumed procession,
For such the angels go,
Rank after rank, with even feet
And uniforms of snow.

17

WHEN night is almost done,
And sunrise grows so near
That we can touch the spaces,
It's time to smooth the hair

And get the dimples ready,
And wonder we could care
For that old faded midnight
That frightened but an hour.

18

READ, sweet, how others strove,
Till we are stouter;
What they renounced,
Till we are less afraid;
How many times they bore
The faithful witness,
Till we are helped,
As if a kingdom cared!

Read then of faith
That shone above the fagot;
Clear strains of hymn
The river could not drown;
Brave names of men
And celestial women,
Passed out of record
Into renown!

19

PAIN has an element of blank;
It cannot recollect
When it began, or if there were
A day when it was not.

It has no future but itself,
Its infinite realms contain
Its past, enlightened to perceive
New periods of pain.

20

I TASTE a liquor never brewed,
From tankards scooped in pearl;
Not all the vats upon the Rhine
Yield such an alcohol!

Inebriate of air am I,
And debauchee of dew,
Reeling, through endless summer days,
From inns of molten blue.

When landlords turn the drunken bee
Out of the foxglove's door,
When butterflies renounce their drams,
I shall but drink the more!

Till seraphs swing their snowy hats,
And saints to windows run,
To see the little tippler
Leaning against the sun!

21

HE ate and drank the precious words,
His spirit grew robust;
He knew no more that he was poor,

Nor that his frame was dust.
He danced along the dingy days,
And this bequest of wings
Was but a book. What liberty
A loosened spirit brings!

22

I HAD no time to hate, because
The grave would hinder me,
And life was not so ample I
Could finish enmity.

Nor had I time to love; but since
Some industry must be,
The little toil of love, I thought,
Was large enough for me.

23

'TWAS such a little, little boat
That toddled down the bay!
'Twas such a gallant, gallant sea
That beckoned it away!

'Twas such a greedy, greedy wave
That licked it from the coast;
Nor ever guessed the stately sails
My little craft was lost!

24

WHETHER my bark went down at sea,
Whether she met with gales,

Whether to isles enchanted
She bent her docile sails;

By what mystic mooring
She is held to-day,—
This is the errand of the eye
Out upon the bay.

25

BELSHAZZAR had a letter,—
He never had but one;
Belshazzar's correspondent
Concluded and begun
In that immortal copy
The conscience of us all
Can read without its glasses
On revelation's wall.

26

THE brain within its groove
Runs evenly and true;
But let a splinter swerve,
'Twere easier for you
To put the water back
When floods have slit the hills,
And scooped a turnpike for themselves,
And blotted out the mills!

27

I'M nobody! Who are you?
Are you nobody, too?

[15]

Then there's a pair of us—don't tell!
They'd banish us, you know.

How dreary to be somebody!
How public, like a frog
To tell your name the livelong day
To an admiring bog!

28

I BRING an unaccustomed wine
To lips long parching, next to mine,
And summon them to drink.

Crackling with fever, they essay;
I turn my brimming eyes away,
And come next hour to look.

The hands still hug the tardy glass;
The lips I would have cooled, alas!
Are so superfluous cold,

I would as soon attempt to warm
The bosoms where the frost has lain
Ages beneath the mould.

Some other thirsty there may be
To whom this would have pointed me
Had it remained to speak.

And so I always bear the cup
If, haply, mine may be the drop
Some pilgrim thirst to slake,—

[16]

If, haply, any say to me,
"Unto the little, unto me,"
When I at last awake.

29

THE nearest dream recedes, unrealized.
    The heaven we chase
    Like the June bee
    Before the school-boy
    Invites the race,
    Stoops to an easy clover—
Dips—evades—teases—deploys;
    Then to the royal clouds
    Lifts his light pinnace
    Heedless of the boy
Staring, bewildered, at the mocking sky.

    Homesick for steadfast honey,
    Ah! the bee flies not
That brews that rare variety.

30

WE play at paste,
Till qualified for pearl,
Then drop the paste,
And deem ourself a fool.
The shapes, though, were similar,
And our new hands
Learned gem-tactics
Practising sands.

[17]

I found the phrase to every thought
I ever had, but one;
And that defies me,—as a hand
Did try to chalk the sun

To races nurtured in the dark;—
How would your own begin?
Can blaze be done in cochineal,
Or noon in mazarin?

Hope is the thing with feathers
That perches in the soul,
And sings the tune without the words
And never stops at all,

And sweetest in the gale is heard;
And sore must be the storm
That could abash the little bird
That kept so many warm.

I've heard it in the chillest land,
And on the strangest sea;
Yet, never, in extremity,
It asked a crumb of me.

Dare you see a soul at the white heat?
  Then crouch within the door.

Red is the fire's common tint;
    But when the vivid ore

Has sated flame's conditions,
    Its quivering substance plays
Without a color but the light
    Of unanointed blaze.

Least village boasts its blacksmith,
    Whose anvil's even din
Stands symbol for the finer forge
    That soundless tugs within,

Refining these impatient ores
    With hammer and with blaze,
Until the designated light
    Repudiate the forge.

34

Who never lost, are unprepared
A coronet to find;
Who never thirsted, flagons
And cooling tamarind.

Who never climbed the weary league—
Can such a foot explore
The purple territories
On Pizarro's shore?

How many legions overcome?
The emperor will say.

How many colors taken
On Revolution Day?

How many bullets bearest?
The royal scar hast thou?
Angels, write "Promoted"
On this soldier's brow!

35

I CAN wade grief,
Whole pools of it,—
I'm used to that.
But the least push of joy
Breaks up my feet,
And I tip—drunken.
Let no pebble smile,
'Twas the new liquor,—
That was all!

Power is only pain,
Stranded, through discipline,
Till weights will hang.
Give balm to giants,
And they'll wilt, like men.
Give Himmaleh,—
They'll carry him!

36

I NEVER hear the word "escape"
Without a quicker blood,

[2 0]

A sudden expectation,
A flying attitude.

I never hear of prisons broad
By soldiers battered down,
But I tug childish at my bars,—
Only to fail again!

37

FOR each ecstatic instant
We must an anguish pay
In keen and quivering ratio
To the ecstasy.

For each beloved hour
Sharp pittances of years,
Bitter contested farthings
And coffers heaped with tears.

38

THROUGH the straight pass of suffering
The martyrs even trod,
Their feet upon temptation,
Their faces upon God.

A stately, shriven company;
Convulsion playing round,
Harmless as streaks of meteor
Upon a planet's bound.

Their faith the everlasting troth;
Their expectation fair;
The needle to the north degree
Wades so, through polar air.

39

I MEANT to have but modest needs,
Such as content, and heaven;
Within my income these could lie,
And life and I keep even.

But since the last included both,
It would suffice my prayer
But just for one to stipulate,
And grace would grant the pair.

And so, upon this wise I prayed,—
Great Spirit, give to me
A heaven not so large as yours,
But large enough for me.

A smile suffused Jehovah's face;
The cherubim withdrew;
Grave saints stole out to look at me,
And showed their dimples, too.

I left the place with all my might,—
My prayer away I threw;
The quiet ages picked it up,
And Judgment twinkled, too,

[22]

That one so honest be extant
As take the tale for true
That "Whatsoever you shall ask,
Itself be given you."

But I, grown shrewder, scan the skies
With a suspicious air,—
As children, swindled for the first,
All swindlers be, infer.

40

*T*HE thought beneath so slight a film
Is more distinctly seen,—
As laces just reveal the surge,
Or mists the Apennine.

41

*T*HE soul unto itself
Is an imperial friend,—
Or the most agonizing spy
An enemy could send.

Secure against its own,
No treason it can fear;
Itself its sovereign, of itself
The soul should stand in awe.

42

*S*URGEONS must be very careful
When they take the knife!

Underneath their fine incisions
Stirs the culprit,—Life!

43

J LIKE to see it lap the miles,
And lick the valleys up,
And stop to feed itself at tanks;
And then, prodigious, step

Around a pile of mountains,
And, supercilious, peer
In shanties by the sides of roads;
And then a quarry pare

To fit its sides, and crawl between,
Complaining all the while
In horrid, hooting stanza;
Then chase itself down hill

And neigh like Boanerges;
Then, punctual as a star,
Stop—docile and omnipotent—·
At its own stable door.

44

THE show is not the show,
But they that go.
Menagerie to me
My neighbor be.
Fair play—
Both went to see.

DELIGHT becomes pictorial
When viewed through pain,—
More fair, because impossible
That any gain.

The mountain at a given distance
In amber lies;
Approached, the amber flits a little,—
And that's the skies!

A THOUGHT went up my mind to-day
That I have had before,
But did not finish,—some way back,
I could not fix the year,

Nor where it went, nor why it came
The second time to me,
Nor definitely what it was,
Have I the art to say.

But somewhere in my soul, I know
I've met the thing before;
It just reminded me—'twas all—
And came my way no more.

Is Heaven a physician?
   They say that He can heal;

But medicine posthumous
  Is unavailable.

Is Heaven an exchequer?
  They speak of what we owe;
But that negotiation
  I'm not a party to.

48

THOUGH I get home how late, how late!
So I get home, 'twill compensate.
Better will be the ecstasy
That they have done expecting me,
When, night descending, dumb and dark,
They hear my unexpected knock.
Transporting must the moment be,
Brewed from decades of agony!

To think just how the fire will burn,
Just how long-cheated eyes will turn
To wonder what myself will say,
And what itself will say to me,
Beguiles the centuries of way!

49

A POOR torn heart, a tattered heart,
That sat it down to rest,
Nor noticed that the ebbing day
Flowed silver to the west,
Nor noticed night did soft descend

Nor constellation burn,
Intent upon the vision
Of latitudes unknown.

The angels, happening that way,
This dusty heart espied;
Tenderly took it up from toil
And carried it to God.
There,—sandals for the barefoot;
There,—gathered from the gales,
Do the blue havens by the hand
Lead the wandering sails.

50

I SHOULD have been too glad, I see,
Too lifted for the scant degree
    Of life's penurious round;
My little circuit would have shamed
This new circumference, have blamed
    The homelier time behind.

I should have been too saved, I see,
Too rescued; fear too dim to me
    That I could spell the prayer
I knew so perfect yesterday,—
That scalding one, "Sabachthani,"
    Recited fluent here.

Earth would have been too much, I see,
And heaven not enough for me;
    I should have had the joy

Without the fear to justify,—
The palm without the Calvary;
   So, Saviour, crucify.

Defeat whets victory, they say;
The reefs in old Gethsemane
   Endear the shore beyond.
'Tis beggars banquets best define;
'Tis thirsting vitalizes wine,—
   Faith faints to understand.

51

It tossed and tossed,—
A little brig I knew,—
O'ertook by blast,
It spun and spun,
And groped delirious, for morn.

It slipped and slipped,
As one that drunken stepped;
Its white foot tripped,
Then dropped from sight.

Ah, brig, good-night
To crew and you;
The ocean's heart too smooth, too blue,
To break for you.

52

VICTORY comes late,
And is held low to freezing lips

Too rapt with frost
To take it.

How sweet it would have tasted,
Just a drop!
Was God so economical?
His table's spread too high for us
Unless we dine on tip-toe.
Crumbs fit such little mouths,
Cherries suit robins;
The eagle's golden breakfast
Strangles them.
God keeps his oath to sparrows,
Who of little love
Know how to starve!

53

God gave a loaf to every bird,
But just a crumb to me;
I dare not eat it, though I starve,—
My poignant luxury
To own it, touch it, prove the feat
That made the pellet mine,—
Too happy in my sparrow chance
For ampler coveting.

It might be famine all around,
I could not miss an ear,
Such plenty smiles upon my board,
My garner shows so fair.
I wonder how the rich may feel,—

An Indiaman—an Earl?
I deem that I with but a crumb
Am sovereign of them all.

54

EXPERIMENT to me
Is every one I meet.
If it contain a kernel?
The figure of a nut

Presents upon a tree,
Equally plausibly;
But meat within is requisite,
To squirrels and to me.

55

MY country need not change her gown,
Her triple suit as sweet
As when 'twas cut at Lexington,
And first pronounced "a fit."

Great Britain disapproves "the stars";
Disparagement discreet,—
There's something in their attitude
That taunts her bayonet.

56

FAITH is a fine invention
For gentlemen who see;

But microscopes are prudent
In an emergency!

EXCEPT the heaven had come so near,
So seemed to choose my door,
The distance would not haunt me so;
I had not hoped before.

But just to hear the grace depart
I never thought to see,
Afflicts me with a double loss;
'Tis lost, and lost to me.

PORTRAITS are to daily faces
As an evening west
To a fine, pedantic sunshine
In a satin vest.

I TOOK my power in my hand
And went against the world;
'Twas not so much as David had,
But I was twice as bold.

I aimed my pebble, but myself
Was all the one that fell.
Was it Goliath was too large,
Or only I too small?

[3 1]

A SHADY friend for torrid days
Is easier to find
Than one of higher temperature
For frigid hour of mind.

The vane a little to the east
Scares muslin souls away;
If broadcloth breasts are firmer
Than those of organdy,

Who is to blame? The weaver?
Ah! the bewildering thread!
The tapestries of paradise
So notelessly are made!

ЄACH life converges to some centre
Expressed or still;
Exists in every human nature
A goal,

Admitted scarcely to itself, it may be,
Too fair
For credibility's temerity
To dare.

Adored with caution, as a brittle heaven,
To reach
Were hopeless as the rainbow's raiment
To touch,

Yet persevered toward, surer for the distance;
How high
Unto the saints' slow diligence
The sky!

Ungained, it may be, by life's low venture,
But then,
Eternity enables the endeavoring
Again.

62

BEFORE I got my eye put out,
I liked as well to see
As other creatures that have eyes,
And know no other way.

But were it told to me, to-day,
That I might have the sky
For mine, I tell you that my heart
Would split, for size of me.

The meadows mine, the mountains mine,—
All forests, stintless stars,
As much of noon as I could take
Between my finite eyes.

The motions of the dipping birds,
The lightning's jointed road,
For mine to look at when I liked,—
The news would strike me dead!

So, safer, guess, with just my soul
Upon the window-pane

Where other creatures put their eyes,
Incautious of the sun.

63

TALK with prudence to a beggar
Of "Potosi" and the mines!
Reverently to the hungry
Of your viands and your wines!

Cautious, hint to any captive
You have passed enfranchised feet!
Anecdotes of air in dungeons
Have sometimes proved deadly sweet!

64

HE preached upon "breadth" till it argued him narrow,—
The broad are too broad to define;
And of "truth" until it proclaimed him a liar,—
The truth never flaunted a sign.

Simplicity fled from his counterfeit presence
As gold the pyrites would shun.
What confusion would cover the innocent Jesus
To meet so enabled a man!

65

GOOD night! which put the candle out?
A jealous zephyr, not a doubt.
   Ah! friend, you little knew
How long at that celestial wick

The angels labored diligent;
    Extinguished, now, for you!

It might have been the lighthouse spark
Some sailor, rowing in the dark,
    Had importuned to see!
It might have been the waning lamp
That lit the drummer from the camp
    To purer reveille!

66

WHEN I hoped I feared,
Since I hoped I dared;
Everywhere alone
As a church remain;
Spectre cannot harm,
Serpent cannot charm;
He deposes doom,
Who hath suffered him.

67

A DEED knocks first at thought,
And then it knocks at will.
That is the manufacturing spot,
And will at home and well.

It then goes out an act,
Or is entombed so still
That only to the ear of God
Its doom is audible.

[35]

MINE enemy is growing old,—
I have at last revenge.
The palate of the hate departs;
If any would avenge,—

Let him be quick, the viand flits,
It is a faded meat.
Anger as soon as fed is dead;
'Tis starving makes it fat.

REMORSE is memory awake,
Her companies astir,—
A presence of departed acts
At window and at door.

Its past set down before the soul,
And lighted with a match,
Perusal to facilitate
Of its condensed despatch.

Remorse is cureless,—the disease
Not even God can heal;
For 'tis His institution,—
The complement of hell.

THE body grows outside,—
The more convenient way,—

That if the spirit like to hide,
Its temple stands alway

Ajar, secure, inviting;
It never did betray
The soul that asked its shelter
In timid honesty.

71

UNDUE significance a starving man attaches
To food
Far off; he sighs, and therefore hopeless,
And therefore good.

Partaken, it relieves indeed, but proves us
That spices fly
In the receipt. It was the distance
Was savory.

72

HEART not so heavy as mine,
Wending late home,
As it passed my window
Whistled itself a tune,—

A careless snatch, a ballad,
A ditty of the street;
Yet to my irritated ear
An anodyne so sweet,

It was as if a bobolink,
Sauntering this way,

Carolled and mused and carolled,
Then bubbled slow away.

It was as if a chirping brook
Upon a toilsome way
Set bleeding feet to minuets
Without the knowing why.

To-morrow, night will come again,
Weary, perhaps, and sore.
Ah, bugle, by my window,
I pray you stroll once more!

73

I MANY times thought peace had come,
When peace was far away;
As wrecked men deem they sight the land
At centre of the sea,

And struggle slacker, but to prove,
As hopelessly as I,
How many the fictitious shores
Before the harbor lie.

74

UNTO my books so good to turn
Far ends of tired days;
It half endears the abstinence,
And pain is missed in praise.

As flavors cheer retarded guests
With banquetings to be,

So spices stimulate the time
Till my small library.

It may be wilderness without,
Far feet of failing men,
But holiday excludes the night,
And it is bells within.

I thank these kinsmen of the shelf;
Their countenances bland
Enamour in prospective,
And satisfy, obtained.

75

THIS merit hath the worst,—
It cannot be again.
When Fate hath taunted last
And thrown her furthest stone,

The maimed may pause and breathe,
And glance securely round.
The deer invites no longer
Than it eludes the hound.

76

I HAD been hungry all the years;
My noon had come, to dine;
I, trembling, drew the table near,
And touched the curious wine.

'Twas this on tables I had seen,
When turning, hungry, lone,

I looked in windows, for the wealth
I could not hope to own.

I did not know the ample bread,
'Twas so unlike the crumb
The birds and I had often shared
In Nature's dining-room.

The plenty hurt me, 'twas so new,—
Myself felt ill and odd,
As berry of a mountain bush
Transplanted to the road.

Nor was I hungry; so I found
That hunger was a way
Of persons outside windows,
The entering takes away.

77

I GAINED it so,
By climbing slow,
By catching at the twigs that grow
Between the bliss and me.
It hung so high,
As well the sky
Attempt by strategy.

I said I gained it,—
This was all.
Look, how I clutch it,
Lest it fall,

And I a pauper go;
Unfitted by an instant's grace
For the contented beggar's face
I wore an hour ago.

78

To learn the transport by the pain,
As blind men learn the sun;
To die of thirst, suspecting
That brooks in meadows run;

To stay the homesick, homesick feet
Upon a foreign shore
Haunted by native lands, the while,
And blue, beloved air—

This is the sovereign anguish,
This, the signal woe!
These are the patient laureates
Whose voices, trained below,

Ascend in ceaseless carol,
Inaudible, indeed,
To us, the duller scholars
Of the mysterious bard!

79

I years had been from home,
And now, before the door,
I dared not open, lest a face
I never saw before

Stare vacant into mine
And ask my business there.
My business,—just a life I left,
Was such still dwelling there?

I fumbled at my nerve,
I scanned the windows near;
The silence like an ocean rolled,
And broke against my ear.

I laughed a wooden laugh
That I could fear a door,
Who danger and the dead had faced,
But never quaked before.

I fitted to the latch
My hand, with trembling care,
Lest back the awful door should spring,
And leave me standing there.

I moved my fingers off
As cautiously as glass,
And held my ears, and like a thief
Fled gasping from the house.

80

PRAYER is the little implement
Through which men reach
Where presence is denied them.
They fling their speech

By means of it in God's ear;
If then He hear,

[4 2]

This sums the apparatus
Comprised in prayer.

81

I KNOW that he exists
Somewhere, in silence.
He has hid his rare life
From our gross eyes.

'Tis in instant's play,
'Tis a fond ambush,
Just to make bliss
Earn her own surprise!

But should the play
Prove piercing earnest,
Should the glee glaze
In death's stiff stare,

Would not the fun
Look too expensive?
Would not the jest
Have crawled too far?

82

MUSICIANS wrestle everywhere:
All day, among the crowded air,
   I hear the silver strife;
And—waking long before the dawn—
Such transport breaks upon the town
   I think it that "new life"!

[43]

It is not bird, it has no nest;
Nor band, in brass and scarlet dressed,
    Nor tambourine, nor man;
It is not hymn from pulpit read,—
The morning stars the treble led
    On time's first afternoon!

Some say it is the spheres at play!
Some say that bright majority
    Of vanished dames and men!
Some think it service in the place
Where we, with late, celestial face,
    Please God, shall ascertain!

83

Just lost when I was saved!
Just felt the world go by!
Just girt me for the onset with eternity,
When breath blew back,
And on the other side
I heard recede the disappointed tide!

Therefore, as one returned, I feel,
Odd secrets of the line to tell!
Some sailor, skirting foreign shores,
Some pale reporter from the awful doors
Before the seal!

Next time, to stay!
Next time, the things to see
By ear unheard,
Unscrutinized by eye.

Next time, to tarry,
While the ages steal,—
Slow tramp the centuries,
And the cycles wheel.

84

'Tis little I could care for pearls
    Who own the ample sea;
Or brooches, when the Emperor
    With rubies pelteth me;

Or gold, who am the Prince of Mines;
    Or diamonds, when I see
A diadem to fit a dome
    Continual crowning me.

85

Superiority to fate
    Is difficult to learn.
'Tis not conferred by any,
    But possible to earn

A pittance at a time,
    Until, to her surprise,
The soul with strict economy
    Subsists till Paradise.

86

Hope is a subtle glutton;
    He feeds upon the fair;

And yet, inspected closely,
   What abstinence is there!

His is the halcyon table
   That never seats but one,
And whatsoever is consumed
   The same amounts remain.

87

FORBIDDEN fruit a flavor has
   That lawful orchards mocks;
How luscious lies the pea within
   The pod that Duty locks!

88

HEAVEN is what I cannot reach!
   The apple on the tree,
Provided it do hopeless hang,
   That "heaven" is, to me.

The color on the cruising cloud,
   The interdicted ground
Behind the hill, the house behind,—
   There Paradise is found!

89

A WORD is dead
When it is said,
   Some say.
I say it just

Begins to live
  That day.

To venerate the simple days
  Which lead the seasons by,
Needs but to remember
  That from you or me
They may take the trifle
  Termed mortality!

To invest existence with a stately air,
Needs but to remember
  That the acorn there
Is the egg of forests
  For the upper air!

It's such a little thing to weep,
  So short a thing to sigh;
And yet by trades the size of these
  We men and women die!

Drowning is not so pitiful
  As the attempt to rise.
Three times, 'tis said, a sinking man
  Comes up to face the skies,
And then declines forever
  To that abhorred abode

Where hope and he part company,—
   For he is grasped of God.
The Maker's cordial visage,
   However good to see,
Is shunned, we must admit it,
   Like an adversity.

93

How still the bells in steeples stand,
   Till, swollen with the sky,
They leap upon their silver feet
   In frantic melody!

94

COULD any mortal lip divine
   The undeveloped freight
Of a delivered syllable,
   'Twould crumble with the weight.

95

MY life closed twice before its close;
   It yet remains to see
If Immortality unveil
   A third event to me,

So huge, so hopeless to conceive,
   As these that twice befell.
Parting is all we know of heaven,
   And all we need of hell.

[48]

WE never know how high we are
　　Till we are called to rise;
And then, if we are true to plan,
　　Our statures touch the skies.

The heroism we recite
　　Would be a daily thing,
Did not ourselves the cubits warp
　　For fear to be a king.

WHILE I was fearing it, it came,
　　But came with less of fear,
Because that fearing it so long
　　Had almost made it dear.
There is a fitting a dismay,
　　A fitting a despair.
'Tis harder knowing it is due,
　　Than knowing it is here.
The trying on the utmost,
　　The morning it is new,
Is terribler than wearing it
　　A whole existence through.

THERE is no frigate like a book
　　To take us lands away,
Nor any coursers like a page
　　Of prancing poetry.

This traverse may the poorest take
    Without oppress of toll;
How frugal is the chariot
    That bears a human soul!

99

WHO has not found the heaven below
    Will fail of it above.
God's residence is next to mine,
    His furniture is love.

100

A FACE devoid of love or grace,
A hateful, hard, successful face,
    A face with which a stone
Would feel as thoroughly at ease
As were they old acquaintances,—
    First time together thrown.

101

I HAD a guinea golden;
    I lost it in the sand,
And though the sum was simple,
    And pounds were in the land,
Still had it such a value
    Unto my frugal eye,
That when I could not find it
    I sat me down to sigh.

I had a crimson robin
 Who sang full many a day,
But when the woods were painted
 He, too, did fly away.
Time brought me other robins,—
 Their ballads were the same,—
Still for my missing troubadour
 I kept the "house at hame."

I had a star in heaven;
 One Pleiad was its name,
And when I was not heeding
 It wandered from the same.
And though the skies are crowded,
 And all the night ashine,
I do not care about it,
 Since none of them are mine.

My story has a moral:
 I have a missing friend,—
Pleiad its name, and robin,
 And guinea in the sand,—
And when this mournful ditty,
 Accompanied with tear,
Shall meet the eye of traitor
 In country far from here,
Grant that repentance solemn
 May seize upon his mind,
And he no consolation
 Beneath the sun may find.

FROM all the jails the boys and girls
  Ecstatically leap,—
Beloved, only afternoon
  That prison doesn't keep.

They storm the earth and stun the air,
  A mob of solid bliss.
Alas! that frowns could lie in wait
  For such a foe as this!

FEW get enough,—enough is one,
  To that ethereal throng
Have not each one of us the right
  To stealthily belong?

I FELT a cleavage in my mind
  As if my brain had split;
I tried to match it, seam by seam,
  But could not make them fit.

The thought behind I strove to join
  Unto the thought before,
But sequence ravelled out of reach
  Like balls upon a floor.

THE reticent volcano keeps
  His never slumbering plan;

[52]

Confided are his projects pink
    To no precarious man.

If nature will not tell the tale
    Jehovah told to her,
Can human nature not survive
    Without a listener?

Admonished by her buckled lips
    Let every babbler be.
The only secret people keep
    Is Immortality.

106

IF recollecting were forgetting,
    Then I remember not;
And if forgetting, recollecting,
    How near I had forgot!
And if to miss were merry,
    And if to mourn were gay,
How very blithe the fingers
    That gathered these to-day!

107

THE farthest thunder that I heard
    Was nearer than the sky,
And rumbles still, though torrid noons
    Have lain their missiles by.
The lightning that preceded it
    Struck no one but myself,
But I would not exchange the bolt

For all the rest of life.
Indebtedness to oxygen
    The chemist may repay,
But not the obligation
    To electricity.
It founds the homes and decks the days,
    And every clamor bright
Is but the gleam concomitant
    Of that waylaying light.
The thought is quiet as a flake,—
    A crash without a sound;
How life's reverberation
    Its explanation found!

108

ON the bleakness of my lot
    Bloom I strove to raise.
Late, my acre of a rock
    Yielded grape and maize.

Soil of flint if steadfast tilled
    Will reward the hand;
Seed of palm by Lybian sun
    Fructified in sand.

109

A DOOR just opened on a street—
    I, lost, was passing by—
An instant's width of warmth disclosed,
    And wealth, and company.

The door as sudden shut, and I,
    I, lost, was passing by,—
Lost doubly, but by contrast most,
    Enlightening misery.

110

Are friends delight or pain?
Could bounty but remain
    Riches were good.

But if they only stay
Bolder to fly away,
    Riches are sad.

111

Fate slew him, but he did not drop;
    She felled—he did not fall—
Impaled him on her fiercest stakes—
    He neutralized them all.

She stung him, sapped his firm advance,
    But, when her worst was done,
And he, unmoved, regarded her,
    Acknowledged him a man.

112

I measure every grief I meet
    With analytic eyes;
I wonder if it weighs like mine,
    Or has an easier size.

[55]

I wonder if they bore it long,
    Or did it just begin?
I could not tell the date of mine,
    It feels so old a pain.

I wonder if it hurts to live,
    And if they have to try,
And whether, could they choose between,
    They would not rather die.

I wonder if when years have piled—
    Some thousands—on the cause
Of early hurt, if such a lapse
    Could give them any pause;

Or would they go on aching still
    Through centuries above,
Enlightened to a larger pain
    By contrast with the love.

The grieved are many, I am told;
    The reason deeper lies,—
Death is but one and comes but once,
    And only nails the eyes.

There's grief of want, and grief of cold,—
    A sort they call "despair";
There's banishment from native eyes,
    In sight of native air.

And though I may not guess the kind
    Correctly, yet to me
A piercing comfort it affords
    In passing Calvary,

To note the fashions of the cross,
    Of those that stand alone,
Still fascinated to presume
    That some are like my own.

113

J HAVE a king who does not speak
So, wondering, thro' the hours meek
    I trudge the day away,—
Half glad when it is night and sleep,
If, haply, thro' a dream to peep
    In parlors shut by day.

And if I do, when morning comes,
It is as if a hundred drums
    Did round my pillow roll,
And shouts fill all my childish sky,
And bells keep saying "victory"
    From steeples in my soul!

And if I don't, the little Bird
Within the Orchard is not heard,
    And I omit to pray,
"Father, thy will be done" to-day,
For my will goes the other way,
    And it were perjury!

114

JT dropped so low in my regard
    I heard it hit the ground,

And go to pieces on the stones
    At bottom of my mind;

Yet blamed the fate that fractured, less
    Than I reviled myself
For entertaining plated wares
    Upon my silver shelf.

115

To lose one's faith surpasses
    The loss of an estate,
Because estates can be
    Replenished,—faith cannot.

Inherited with life,
    Belief but once can be;
Annihilate a single clause,
    And Being's beggary.

116

I HAD a daily bliss
    I half indifferent viewed,
Till sudden I perceived it stir,—
    It grew as I pursued,

Till when, around a crag,
    It wasted from my sight,
Enlarged beyond my utmost scope,
    I learned its sweetness right.

LIFE, and Death, and Giants
Such as these, are still.
Minor apparatus, hopper of the mill,
Beetle at the candle,
Or a fife's small fame,
Maintain by accident
That they proclaim.

OUR lives are Swiss,—
So still, so cool,
Till, some odd afternoon,
The Alps neglect their curtains,
And we look farther on.

Italy stands the other side,
While, like a guard between,
The solemn Alps,
The siren Alps,
Forever intervene!

REMEMBRANCE has a rear and front,—
'Tis something like a house;
It has a garret also
For refuge and the mouse,

Besides, the deepest cellar
That ever mason hewed;

[59]

Look to it, by its fathoms
    Ourselves be not pursued.

120

To hang our head ostensibly,
    And subsequent to find
That such was not the posture
    Of our immortal mind,

Affords the sly presumption
    That, in so dense a fuzz,
You, too, take cobweb attitudes
    Upon a plane of gauze!

121

THE brain is wider than the sky,
    For, put them side by side,
The one the other will include
    With ease, and you beside.

The brain is deeper than the sea,
    For, hold them, blue to blue,
The one the other will absorb,
    As sponges, buckets do.

The brain is just the weight of God,
    For, lift them, pound for pound,
And they will differ, if they do,
    As syllable from sound.

THE past is such a curious creature,
  To look her in the face
A transport may reward us,
  Or a disgrace.

Unarmed if any meet her,
  I charge him, fly!
Her rusty ammunition
  Might yet reply!

To help our bleaker parts
  Salubrious hours are given,
Which if they do not fit for earth
  Drill silently for heaven.

WHAT soft, cherubic creatures
  These gentlewomen are!
One would as soon assault a plush
  Or violate a star.

Such dimity convictions,
  A horror so refined
Of freckled human nature,
  Of Deity ashamed,—

It's such a common glory,
  A fisherman's degree!

Redemption, brittle lady,
    Be so ashamed of thee.

125

Iᴛ might be easier
    To fail with land in sight,
Than gain my blue peninsula
    To perish of delight.

126

I sᴛᴇᴘᴘᴇᴅ from plank to plank
    So slow and cautiously;
The stars about my head I felt,
    About my feet the sea.

I knew not but the next
    Would be my final inch,—
This gave me that precarious gait
    Some call experience.

127

Sᴏғᴛᴇɴᴇᴅ by Time's consummate plush,
    How sleek the woe appears
That threatened childhood's citadel
    And undermined the years!

Bisected now by bleaker griefs,
    We envy the despair
That devastated childhood's realm,
    So easy to repair.

PART TWO

NATURE

My nosegays are for captives,
   Dim, long-expectant eyes,
Fingers denied the plucking,
   Patient till paradise.

To such, if they should whisper
   Of morning and the moor,
They bear no other errand,
   And I, no other prayer.

NATURE, the gentlest mother,
Impatient of no child,
The feeblest or the waywardest,—
Her admonition mild

In forest and the hill
By traveller is heard,
Restraining rampant squirrel
Or too impetuous bird.

How fair her conversation,
A summer afternoon,—
Her household, her assembly;
And when the sun goes down

Her voice among the aisles
Incites the timid prayer
Of the minutest cricket,
The most unworthy flower.

When all the children sleep
She turns as long away
As will suffice to light her lamps;
Then, bending from the sky,

With infinite affection
And infiniter care,
Her golden finger on her lip,
Wills silence everywhere.

WILL there really be a morning?
Is there such a thing as day?
Could I see it from the mountains
If I were as tall as they?

Has it feet like water-lilies?
Has it feathers like a bird?
Is it brought from famous countries
Of which I have never heard?

Oh, some scholar! Oh, some sailor!
Oh, some wise man from the skies!
Please to tell a little pilgrim
Where the place called morning lies!

AT half-past three a single bird
Unto a silent sky
Propounded but a single term
Of cautious melody.

At half-past four, experiment
Had subjugated test,
And lo! her silver principle
Supplanted all the rest.

At half-past seven, element
Nor implement was seen,
And place was where the presence was,
Circumference between.

*T*HE day came slow, till five o'clock,
Then sprang before the hills
Like hindered rubies, or the light
A sudden musket spills.

The purple could not keep the east,
The sunrise shook from fold,
Like breadths of topaz, packed a night,
The lady just unrolled.

The happy winds their timbrels took;
The birds, in docile rows,
Arranged themselves around their prince—
(The wind is prince of those).

The orchard sparkled like a Jew,—
How mighty 'twas, to stay
A guest in this stupendous place,
The parlor of the day!

5

*T*HE sun just touched the morning;
The morning, happy thing,
Supposed that he had come to dwell,
And life would be all spring.

She felt herself supremer,—
A raised, ethereal thing;
Henceforth for her what holiday!
Meanwhile, her wheeling king

Trailed slow along the orchards
His haughty, spangled hems,
Leaving a new necessity,—
The want of diadems!

The morning fluttered, staggered,
Felt feebly for her crown,—
Her unanointed forehead
Henceforth her only one.

6

THE robin is the one
That interrupts the morn
With hurried, few, express reports
When March is scarcely on.

The robin is the one
That overflows the noon
With her cherubic quantity,
An April but begun.

The robin is the one
That speechless from her nest
Submits that home and certainty
And sanctity are best.

7

FROM cocoon forth a butterfly
As lady from her door
Emerged—a summer afternoon—
Repairing everywhere,

Without design, that I could trace,
Except to stray abroad
On miscellaneous enterprise
The clovers understood.

Her pretty parasol was seen
Contracting in a field
Where men made hay, then struggling hard
With an opposing cloud,

Where parties, phantom as herself,
To Nowhere seemed to go
In purposeless circumference,
As 'twere a tropic show.

And notwithstanding bee that worked,
And flower that zealous blew,
This audience of idleness
Disdained them, from the sky,

Till sundown crept, a steady tide,
And men that made the hay,
And afternoon, and butterfly,
Extinguished in its sea.

8

BEFORE you thought of spring,
Except as a surmise,
You see, God bless his suddenness,
A fellow in the skies
Of independent hues,

A little weather-worn,
Inspiriting habiliments
Of indigo and brown.

With specimens of song,
As if for you to choose,
Discretion in the interval,
With gay delays he goes
To some superior tree
Without a single leaf,
And shouts for joy to nobody
But his seraphic self!

⁹

An altered look about the hills;
A Tyrian light the village fills;
A wider sunrise in the dawn;
A deeper twilight on the lawn;
A print of a vermilion foot;
A purple finger on the slope;
A flippant fly upon the pane;
A spider at his trade again;
An added strut in chanticleer;
A flower expected everywhere;
An axe shrill singing in the woods;
Fern-odors on untravelled roads,—
All this, and more I cannot tell,
A furtive look you know as well,
And Nicodemus' mystery
Receives its annual reply.

"Whose are the little beds," I asked,
"Which in the valleys lie?"
Some shook their heads, and others smiled,
And no one made reply.

"Perhaps they did not hear," I said;
"I will inquire again.
Whose are the beds, the tiny beds
So thick upon the plain?"

" 'Tis daisy in the shortest;
A little farther on,
Nearest the door to wake the first,
Little leontodon.

" 'Tis iris, sir, and aster,
Anemone and bell,
Batschia in the blanket red,
And chubby daffodil."

Meanwhile at many cradles
Her busy foot she plied,
Humming the quaintest lullaby
That ever rocked a child.

"Hush! Epigea wakens!
The crocus stirs her lids,
Rhodora's cheek is crimson,—
She's dreaming of the woods."

Then, turning from them, reverent,
"Their bed-time 'tis," she said;

"The bumble-bees will wake them
When April woods are red."

PIGMY seraphs gone astray,
Velvet people from Vevay,
Belles from some lost summer day,
Bees' exclusive coterie.
Paris could not lay the fold
Belted down with emerald;
Venice could not show a cheek
Of a tint so lustrous meek.
Never such an ambuscade
As of brier and leaf displayed
For my little damask maid.
I had rather wear her grace
Than an earl's distinguished face;

I had rather dwell like her
Than be Duke of Exeter,
Royalty enough for me
To subdue the bumble-bee!

12

To hear an oriole sing
May be a common thing,
Or only a divine.

It is not of the bird
Who sings the same, unheard,
As unto crowd.

The fashion of the ear
Attireth that it hear
In dun or fair.

So whether it be rune,
Or whether it be none,
Is of within;

The "tune is in the tree,"
The sceptic showeth me;
"No, sir! In thee!"

13

ONE of the ones that Midas touched,
Who failed to touch us all,
Was that confiding prodigal,
The blissful oriole.

So drunk, he disavows it
With badinage divine;
So dazzling, we mistake him
For an alighting mine.

A pleader, a dissembler,
An epicure, a thief,—
Betimes an oratorio,
An ecstasy in chief;

The Jesuit of orchards,
He cheats as he enchants
Of an entire attar
For his decamping wants.

The splendor of a Burmah,
The meteor of birds,
Departing like a pageant
Of ballads and of bards.

I never thought that Jason sought
For any golden fleece;
But then I am a rural man,
With thoughts that make for peace.

But if there were a Jason,
Tradition suffer me
Behold his lost emolument
Upon the apple-tree.

14

I DREADED that first robin so,
But he is mastered now,
And I'm accustomed to him grown,—
He hurts a little, though.

I thought if I could only live
Till that first shout got by,
Not all pianos in the woods
Had power to mangle me.

I dared not meet the daffodils,
For fear their yellow gown
Would pierce me with a fashion
So foreign to my own.

I wished the grass would hurry,
So when 'twas time to see,

He'd be too tall, the tallest one
Could stretch to look at me.

I could not bear the bees should come,
I wished they'd stay away
In those dim countries where they go:
What word had they for me?

They're here, though; not a creature failed,
No blossom stayed away
In gentle deference to me,
The Queen of Calvary.

Each one salutes me as he goes,
And I my childish plumes
Lift, in bereaved acknowledgment
Of their unthinking drums.

15

A ROUTE of evanescence
With a revolving wheel;
A resonance of emerald,
A rush of cochineal;
And every blossom on the bush
Adjusts its tumbled head,—
The mail from Tunis, probably,
An easy morning's ride.

16

*T*HE skies can't keep their secret!
They tell it to the hills—

The hills just tell the orchards—
And they the daffodils!

A bird, by chance, that goes that way
Soft overheard the whole.
If I should bribe the little bird,
Who knows but she would tell?

I think I won't, however,
It's finer not to know;
If summer were an axiom,
What sorcery had snow?

So keep your secret, Father!
I would not, if I could,
Know what the sapphire fellows do,
In your new-fashioned world!

17

Who robbed the woods,
The trusting woods?
The unsuspecting trees
Brought out their burrs and mosses
His fantasy to please.
He scanned their trinkets, curious,
He grasped, he bore away.
What will the solemn hemlock,
What will the fir-tree say?

18

Two butterflies went out at noon
And waltzed above a stream,

Then stepped straight through the firmament
And rested on a beam;

And then together bore away
Upon a shining sea,—
Though never yet, in any port,
Their coming mentioned be.

If spoken by the distant bird,
If met in ether sea
By frigate or by merchantman,
Report was not to me.

19

I STARTED early, took my dog,
And visited the sea;
The mermaids in the basement
Came out to look at me,

And frigates in the upper floor
Extended hempen hands,
Presuming me to be a mouse
Aground, upon the sands.

But no man moved me till the tide
Went past my simple shoe,
And past my apron and my belt,
And past my bodice too,

And made as he would eat me up
As wholly as a dew

Upon a dandelion's sleeve—
And then I started too.

And he—he followed close behind;
I felt his silver heel
Upon my ankle,—then my shoes
Would overflow with pearl.

Until we met the solid town,
No man he seemed to know;
And bowing with a mighty look
At me, the sea withdrew.

20

ARCTURUS is his other name,—
I'd rather call him star!
It's so unkind of science
To go and interfere!

I pull a flower from the woods,—
A monster with a glass
Computes the stamens in a breath,
And has her in a class.

Whereas I took the butterfly
Aforetime in my hat,
He sits erect in cabinets,
The clover-bells forgot.

What once was heaven, is zenith now.
Where I proposed to go

When time's brief masquerade was done,
Is mapped, and charted too!

What if the poles should frisk about
And stand upon their heads!
I hope I'm ready for the worst,
Whatever prank betides!

Perhaps the kingdom of Heaven's changed!
I hope the children there
Won't be new-fashioned when I come,
And laugh at me, and stare!

I hope the father in the skies
Will lift his little girl,—
Old-fashioned, naughty, everything,—
Over the stile of pearl!

21

An awful tempest mashed the air,
The clouds were gaunt and few;
A black, as of a spectre's cloak,
Hid heaven and earth from view.

The creatures chuckled on the roofs
And whistled in the air,
And shook their fists and gnashed their teeth,
And swung their frenzied hair.

The morning lit, the birds arose;
The monster's faded eyes

Turned slowly to his native coast,
And peace was Paradise!

22

An everywhere of silver,
With ropes of sand
To keep it from effacing
The track called land.

23

A BIRD came down the walk:
He did not know I saw;
He bit an angle-worm in halves
And ate the fellow, raw.

And then he drank a dew
From a convenient grass,
And then hopped sidewise to the wall
To let a beetle pass.

He glanced with rapid eyes
That hurried all abroad,—
They looked like frightened beads, I thought
He stirred his velvet head

Like one in danger; cautious,
I offered him a crumb,
And he unrolled his feathers
And rowed him softer home

Than oars divide the ocean,
Too silver for a seam,

Or butterflies, off banks of noon,
Leap, plashless, as they swim.

A NARROW fellow in the grass
Occasionally rides;
You may have met him,—did you not?
His notice sudden is.

The grass divides as with a comb,
A spotted shaft is seen;
And then it closes at your feet
And opens further on.

He likes a boggy acre,
A floor too cool for corn.
Yet when a child, and barefoot,
I more than once, at morn,

Have passed, I thought, a whip-lash
Unbraiding in the sun,—
When, stooping to secure it,
It wrinkled, and was gone.

Several of nature's people
I know, and they know me;
I feel for them a transport
Of cordiality;

But never met this fellow,
Attended or alone,

Without a tighter breathing,
And zero at the bone.

25

THE mushroom is the elf of plants,
At evening it is not;
At morning in a truffled hut
It stops upon a spot

As if it tarried always;
And yet its whole career
Is shorter than a snake's delay,
And fleeter than a tare.

'Tis vegetation's juggler,
The germ of alibi;
Doth like a bubble antedate,
And like a bubble hie.

I feel as if the grass were pleased
To have it intermit;
The surreptitious scion
Of summer's circumspect.

Had nature any outcast face,
Could she a son contemn,
Had nature an Iscariot,
That mushroom,—it is him.

26

THERE came a wind like a bugle;
It quivered through the grass,

And a green chill upon the heat
So ominous did pass
We barred the windows and the doors
As from an emerald ghost;
The doom's electric moccasin
That very instant passed.
On a strange mob of panting trees,
And fences fled away,

And rivers where the houses ran
The living looked that day.
The bell within the steeple wild
The flying tidings whirled.
How much can come
And much can go,
And yet abide the world!

27

A SPIDER sewed at night
Without a light
Upon an arc of white.
If ruff it was of dame
Or shroud of gnome,
Himself, himself inform.
Of immortality
His strategy
Was physiognomy.

28

I KNOW a place where summer strives
With such a practised frost,

She each year leads her daisies back,
Recording briefly, "Lost."

But when the south wind stirs the pools
And struggles in the lanes,
Her heart misgives her for her vow,
And she pours soft refrains

Into the lap of adamant,
And spices, and the dew,
That stiffens quietly to quartz,
Upon her amber shoe.

29

THE one that could repeat the summer day
Were greater than itself, though he
Minutest of mankind might be.
And who could reproduce the sun,
At period of going down—
The lingering and the stain, I mean—
When Orient has been outgrown,
And Occident becomes unknown,
His name remain.

30

THE wind tapped like a tired man,
And like a host, "Come in,"
I boldly answered; entered then
My residence within

A rapid, footless guest,
To offer whom a chair

Were as impossible as hand
A sofa to the air.

No bone had he to bind him,
His speech was like the push
Of numerous humming-birds at once
From a superior bush.

His countenance a billow,
His fingers, if he pass,
Let go a music, as of tunes
Blown tremulous in glass.

He visited, still flitting;
Then, like a timid man,
Again he tapped—'twas flurriedly—
And I became alone.

31

NATURE rarer uses yellow
    Than another hue;
Saves she all of that for sunsets,—
    Prodigal of blue,

Spending scarlet like a woman,
    Yellow she affords
Only scantly and selectly,
    Like a lover's words.

32

THE leaves, like women, interchange
    Sagacious confidence;

Somewhat of nods, and somewhat of
    Portentous inference,

The parties in both cases
    Enjoining secrecy,—
Inviolable compact
    To notoriety.

33

How happy is the little stone
That rambles in the road alone,
And doesn't care about careers,
And exigencies never fears;
Whose coat of elemental brown
A passing universe put on;
And independent as the sun,
Associates or glows alone,
Fulfilling absolute decree
In casual simplicity.

34

It sounded as if the streets were running,
And then the streets stood still.
Eclipse was all we could see at the window,
And awe was all we could feel.

By and by the boldest stole out of his covert,
To see if time was there.
Nature was in her beryl apron,
Mixing fresher air.

THE rat is the concisest tenant.
He pays no rent,—
Repudiates the obligation,
On schemes intent.

Balking our wit
To sound or circumvent,
Hate cannot harm
A foe so reticent.

Neither decree
Prohibits him,
Lawful as
Equilibrium.

FREQUENTLY the woods are pink,
Frequently are brown;
Frequently the hills undress
Behind my native town.

Oft a head is crested
I was wont to see,
And as oft a cranny
Where it used to be.

And the earth, they tell me,
On its axis turned,—
Wonderful rotation
By but twelve performed!

THE wind begun to rock the grass
With threatening tunes and low,—
He flung a menace at the earth,
A menace at the sky.

The leaves unhooked themselves from trees
And started all abroad;
The dust did scoop itself like hands
And throw away the road.

The wagons quickened on the streets,
The thunder hurried slow;
The lightning showed a yellow beak,
And then a livid claw.

The birds put up the bars to nests,
The cattle fled to barns;
There came one drop of giant rain,
And then, as if the hands

That held the dams had parted hold,
The waters wrecked the sky,
But overlooked my father's house,
Just quartering a tree.

SOUTH winds jostle them,
Bumblebees come,
Hover, hesitate,
Drink, and are gone.

Butterflies pause
On their passage Cashmere;
I, softly plucking,
Present them here!

39

Bring me the sunset in a cup,
Reckon the morning's flagons up,
   And say how many dew;
Tell me how far the morning leaps,
Tell me what time the weaver sleeps
   Who spun the breadths of blue!

Write me how many notes there be
In the new robin's ecstasy
   Among astonished boughs;
How many trips the tortoise makes,
How many cups the bee partakes,—
   The debauchee of dews!

Also, who laid the rainbow's piers,
Also, who leads the docile spheres
   By withes of supple blue?
Whose fingers string the stalactite,
Who counts the wampum of the night,
   To see that none is due?

Who built this little Alban house
And shut the windows down so close
   My spirit cannot see?
Who'll let me out some gala day,

[89]

With implements to fly away,
  Passing pomposity?

SHE sweeps with many-colored brooms,
And leaves the shreds behind;
Oh, housewife in the evening west,
Come back, and dust the pond!

You dropped a purple ravelling in,
You dropped an amber thread;
And now you've littered all the East
With duds of emerald!

And still she plies her spotted brooms,
And still the aprons fly,
Till brooms fade softly into stars—
And then I come away.

41

LIKE mighty footlights burned the red
At bases of the trees,—
The far theatricals of day
Exhibiting to these.

'Twas universe that did applaud
While, chiefest of the crowd,
Enabled by his royal dress,
Myself distinguished God.

42

WHERE ships of purple gently toss
On seas of daffodil,
Fantastic sailors mingle,
And then—the wharf is still.

43

BLAZING in gold and quenching in purple,
Leaping like leopards to the sky,
Then at the feet of the old horizon
Laying her spotted face, to die;

Stooping as low as the kitchen window,
Touching the roof and tinting the barn,
Kissing her bonnet to the meadow,—
And the juggler of day is gone!

44

FARTHER in summer than the birds,
Pathetic from the grass
A minor nation celebrates
Its unobtrusive mass.

No ordinance is seen,
So gradual the grace,
A pensive custom it becomes,
Enlarging loneliness.

Antiquest felt at noon
When August, burning low,

Calls forth this spectral canticle,
Repose to typify.

Remit as yet no grace,
No furrow on the glow,
Yet a druidic difference
Enhances nature now.

45

As imperceptibly as grief
The summer lapsed away,—
Too imperceptible, at last,
To seem like perfidy.

A quietness distilled,
As twilight long begun,
Or Nature, spending with herself
Sequestered afternoon.

The dusk drew earlier in,
The morning foreign shone,—
A courteous, yet harrowing grace,
As guest who would be gone.

And thus, without a wing,
Or service of a keel,
Our summer made her light escape
Into the beautiful.

46

It can't be summer,—that got through;
It's early yet for spring;

[9 2]

There's that long town of white to cross
Before the blackbirds sing.

It can't be dying,—it's too rouge,—
The dead shall go in white.
So sunset shuts my question down
With clasps of chrysolite.

47

THE gentian weaves her fringes,
The maple's loom is red.
My departing blossoms
Obviate parade.

A brief, but patient illness,
An hour to prepare;
And one, below this morning,
Is where the angels are.

It was a short procession,—
The bobolink was there,
An aged bee addressed us,
And then we knelt in prayer.

We trust that she was willing,—
We ask that we may be.
Summer, sister, seraph,
Let us go with thee!

In the name of the bee
And of the butterfly
And of the breeze, amen!

[9 3]

48

GOD made a little gentian;
It tried to be a rose
And failed, and all the summer laughed.
But just before the snows
There came a purple creature
That ravished all the hill;
And summer hid her forehead,
And mockery was still.
The frosts were her condition;
The Tyrian would not come
Until the North evoked it.
"Creator! shall I bloom?"

BESIDES the autumn poets sing,
A few prosaic days
A little this side of the snow
And that side of the haze.

A few incisive mornings,
A few ascetic eves,—
Gone Mr. Bryant's golden-rod,
And Mr. Thomson's sheaves.

Still is the bustle in the brook,
Sealed are the spicy valves;
Mesmeric fingers softly touch
The eyes of many elves.

Perhaps a squirrel may remain,
My sentiments to share.

Grant me, O Lord, a sunny mind,
Thy windy will to bear!

It sifts from leaden sieves,
It powders all the wood,
It fills with alabaster wool
The wrinkles of the road.

It makes an even face
Of mountain and of plain,—
Unbroken forehead from the east
Unto the east again.

It reaches to the fence,
It wraps it, rail by rail,
Till it is lost in fleeces;
It flings a crystal veil

On stump and stack and stem,—
The summer's empty room,
Acres of seams where harvests were,
Recordless, but for them.

It ruffles wrists of posts,
As ankles of a queen,—
Then stills its artisans like ghosts,
Denying they have been.

51

No brigadier throughout the year
So civic as the Jay.

A neighbor and a warrior too,
With shrill felicity

Pursuing winds that censure us
A February day,
The brother of the universe
Was never blown away.

The snow and he are intimate;
I've often seen them play
When heaven looked upon us all
With such severity,

I felt apology were due
To an insulted sky,
Whose pompous frown was nutriment
To their temerity.

The pillow of this daring head
Is pungent evergreens;
His larder—terse and militant—
Unknown, refreshing things;

His character a tonic,
His future a dispute;
Unfair an immortality
That leaves this neighbor out.

52

New feet within my garden go,
New fingers stir the sod;
A troubadour upon the elm
Betrays the solitude.

New children play upon the green,
New weary sleep below;
And still the pensive spring returns,
And still the punctual snow!

53

PINK, small, and punctual,
Aromatic, low,
Covert in April,
Candid in May,

Dear to the moss,
Known by the knoll,
Next to the robin
In every human soul.

Bold little beauty,
Bedecked with thee,
Nature forswears
Antiquity.

(With the first Arbutus.)

54

THE murmur of a bee
A witchcraft yieldeth me.
If any ask me why,
'Twere easier to die
Than tell.

The red upon the hill
Taketh away my will;

If anybody sneer,
Take care, for God is here,
That's all.

The breaking of the day
Addeth to my degree;
If any ask me how,
Artist, who drew me so,
Must tell!

55

PERHAPS you'd like to buy a flower?
But I could never sell.
If you would like to borrow
Until the daffodil

Unties her yellow bonnet
Beneath the village door,
Until the bees, from clover rows
Their hock and sherry draw,

Why, I will lend until just then,
But not an hour more!

56

THE pedigree of honey
Does not concern the bee;
A clover, any time, to him
Is aristocracy.

57

Some keep the Sabbath going to church;
I keep it staying at home,
With a bobolink for a chorister,
And an orchard for a dome.

Some keep the Sabbath in surplice;
I just wear my wings,
And instead of tolling the bell for church,
Our little sexton sings.

God preaches,—a noted clergyman,—
And the sermon is never long;
So instead of getting to heaven at last,
I'm going all along!

The bee is not afraid of me,
I know the butterfly;
The pretty people in the woods
Receive me cordially.

The brooks laugh louder when I come,
The breezes madder play.
Wherefore, mine eyes, thy silver mists?
Wherefore, O summer's day?

Some rainbow coming from the fair!
Some vision of the World Cashmere

I confidently see!
Or else a peacock's purple train,
Feather by feather, on the plain
Fritters itself away!

The dreamy butterflies bestir,
Lethargic pools resume the whir
Of last year's sundered tune.
From some old fortress on the sun
Baronial bees march, one by one,
In murmuring platoon!

The robins stand as thick to-day
As flakes of snow stood yesterday,
On fence and roof and twig.
The orchis binds her feather on
For her old lover, Don the Sun,
Revisiting the bog!

Without commander, countless, still,
The regiment of wood and hill
In bright detachment stand.
Behold! Whose multitudes are these?
The children of whose turbaned seas,
Or what Circassian land?

60

THE grass so little has to do,—
A sphere of simple green,
With only butterflies to brood,
And bees to entertain,

[100]

And stir all day to pretty tunes
The breezes fetch along,
And hold the sunshine in its lap
And bow to everything;

And thread the dews all night, like pearls,
And make itself so fine,—
A duchess were too common
For such a noticing.

And even when it dies, to pass
In odors so divine,
As lowly spices gone to sleep,
Or amulets of pine.

And then to dwell in sovereign barns,
And dream the days away,—
The grass so little has to do,
I wish I were the hay!

A LITTLE road not made of man,
Enabled of the eye,
Accessible to thill of bee,
Or cart of butterfly.

If town it have, beyond itself,
'Tis that I cannot say;
I only sigh,—no vehicle
Bears me along that way.

A DROP fell on the apple tree,
Another on the roof;
A half a dozen kissed the eaves,
And made the gables laugh.

A few went out to help the brook,
That went to help the sea.
Myself conjectured, Were they pearls,
What necklaces could be!

The dust replaced in hoisted roads,
The birds jocoser sung;
The sunshine threw his hat away,
The orchards spangles hung.

The breezes brought dejected lutes,
And bathed them in the glee;
The East put out a single flag,
And signed the fête away.

63

A SOMETHING in a summer's day,
As slow her flambeaux burn away,
Which solemnizes me.

A something in a summer's noon,—
An azure depth, a wordless tune,
Transcending ecstasy.

And still within a summer's night
A something so transporting bright,
I clap my hands to see;

Then veil my too inspecting face,
Lest such a subtle, shimmering grace
Flutter too far for me.

The wizard-fingers never rest,
The purple brook within the breast
Still chafes its narrow bed;

Still rears the East her amber flag,
Guides still the sun along the crag
His caravan of red,

Like flowers that heard the tale of dews,
But never deemed the dripping prize
Awaited their low brows;

Or bees, that thought the summer's name
Some rumor of delirium
No summer could for them;

Or Arctic creature, dimly stirred
By tropic hint,—some travelled bird
Imported to the wood;

Or wind's bright signal to the ear,
Making that homely and severe,
Contented, known, before

The heaven unexpected came,
To lives that thought their worshipping
A too presumptuous psalm.

64

THIS is the land the sunset washes,
These are the banks of the Yellow Sea;
Where it rose, or whither it rushes,
These are the western mystery!

Night after night her purple traffic
Strews the landing with opal bales;
Merchantmen poise upon horizons,
Dip, and vanish with fairy sails.

65

LIKE trains of cars on tracks of plush
I hear the level bee:
A jar across the flowers goes,
Their velvet masonry

Withstands until the sweet assault
Their chivalry consumes,
While he, victorious, tilts away
To vanquish other blooms.

His feet are shod with gauze,
His helmet is of gold;
His breast, a single onyx
With chrysoprase, inlaid.

His labor is a chant,
His idleness a tune;
Oh, for a bee's experience
Of clovers and of noon!

66

THERE is a flower that bees prefer,
And butterflies desire;
To gain the purple democrat
The humming-birds aspire.

And whatsoever insect pass,
A honey bears away
Proportioned to his several dearth
And her capacity.

Her face is rounder than the moon,
And ruddier than the gown
Of orchis in the pasture,
Or rhododendron worn.

She doth not wait for June;
Before the world is green
Her sturdy little countenance
Against the wind is seen,

Contending with the grass,
Near kinsman to herself,
For privilege of sod and sun,
Sweet litigants for life.

And when the hills are full,
And newer fashions blow,
Doth not retract a single spice
For pang of jealousy.

Her public is the noon,
Her providence the sun,
Her progress by the bee proclaimed
In sovereign, swerveless tune.

The bravest of the host,
Surrendering the last,
Nor even of defeat aware
When cancelled by the frost.

67

PRESENTIMENT is that long shadow on the lawn
Indicative that suns go down;
The notice to the startled grass
That darkness is about to pass.

68

As children bid the guest good-night,
And then reluctant turn,
My flowers raise their pretty lips,
Then put their nightgowns on.

As children caper when they wake,
Merry that it is morn,
My flowers from a hundred cribs
Will peep, and prance again.

ANGELS in the early morning
May be seen the dews among,
Stooping, plucking, smiling, flying:
Do the buds to them belong?

Angels when the sun is hottest
May be seen the sands among,
Stooping, plucking, sighing, flying;
Parched the flowers they bear along.

So bashful when I spied her,
So pretty, so ashamed!
So hidden in her leaflets,
Lest anybody find;

So breathless till I passed her,
So helpless when I turned
And bore her, struggling, blushing,
Her simple haunts beyond!

For whom I robbed the dingle,
For whom betrayed the dell,
Many will doubtless ask me,
But I shall never tell!

71

IT makes no difference abroad,
The seasons fit the same,

The mornings blossom into noons,
And split their pods of flame.

Wild-flowers kindle in the woods,
The brooks brag all the day;
No blackbird bates his jargoning
For passing Calvary.

Auto-da-fé and judgment
Are nothing to the bee;
His separation from his rose
To him seems misery.

72

*T*HE mountain sat upon the plain
In his eternal chair,
His observation omnifold,
His inquest everywhere.

The seasons prayed around his knees,
Like children round a sire:
Grandfather of the days is he,
Of dawn the ancestor.

73

I'LL tell you how the sun rose,—
A ribbon at a time.
The steeples swam in amethyst,
The news like squirrels ran.

The hills untied their bonnets,
The bobolinks begun.

Then I said softly to myself,
"That must have been the sun!"

.   .   .   .   .   .

But how he set, I know not.
There seemed a purple stile
Which little yellow boys and girls
Were climbing all the while

Till when they reached the other side,
A dominie in gray
Put gently up the evening bars,
And led the flock away.

74

THE butterfly's assumption-gown,
In chrysoprase apartments hung,
    This afternoon put on.

How condescending to descend,
And be of buttercups the friend
    In a New England town!

75

OF all the sounds despatched abroad,
There's not a charge to me
Like that old measure in the boughs,
That phraseless melody

The wind does, working like a hand
Whose fingers comb the sky,

Then quiver down, with tufts of tune
Permitted gods and me.

Inheritance it is to us
Beyond the art to earn,
Beyond the trait to take away
By robber, since the gain

Is gotten not of fingers,
And inner than the bone,
Hid golden for the whole of days,
And even in the urn

I cannot vouch the merry dust
Do not arise and play
In some odd pattern of its own
Some quainter holiday.

When winds go round and round in bands,
And thrum upon the door,
And birds take places overhead,
To bear them orchestra,

I crave him grace of summer boughs,
If such an outcast be,
Who never heard that fleshless chant
Rise solemn on the tree,

As if some caravan of sound
Off deserts, in the sky,
Had parted rank,
Then knit, and swept
In seamless company.

*A*PPARENTLY with no surprise
To any happy flower,
The frost beheads it at its play
In accidental power.

The blond assassin passes on,
The sun proceeds unmoved
To measure off another day
For an approving God.

'*T*WAS later when the summer went
Than when the cricket came,
And yet we knew that gentle clock
Meant nought but going home.

'Twas sooner when the cricket went
Than when the winter came,
Yet that pathetic pendulum
Keeps esoteric time.

*T*HESE are the days when birds come back,
A very few, a bird or two,
To take a backward look.

These are the days when skies put on
The old, old sophistries of June,—
A blue and gold mistake.

Oh, fraud that cannot cheat the bee,
Almost thy plausibility
Induces my belief,

Till ranks of seeds their witness bear,
And softly through the altered air
Hurries a timid leaf!

Oh, sacrament of summer days,
Oh, last communion in the haze,
Permit a child to join,

Thy sacred emblems to partake,
Thy consecrated bread to break,
Taste thine immortal wine!

79

THE morns are meeker than they were,
The nuts are getting brown;
The berry's cheek is plumper,
The rose is out of town.

The maple wears a gayer scarf,
The field a scarlet gown.
Lest I should be old-fashioned,
I'll put a trinket on.

80

THE sky is low, the clouds are mean,
A travelling flake of snow
Across a barn or through a rut
Debates if it will go.

A narrow wind complains all day
How some one treated him;
Nature, like us, is sometimes caught
Without her diadem.

81

J THINK the hemlock likes to stand
Upon a marge of snow;
It suits his own austerity,
And satisfies an awe

That men must slake in wilderness,
Or in the desert cloy,—
An instinct for the hoar, the bald,
Lapland's necessity.

The hemlock's nature thrives on cold;
The gnash of northern winds
Is sweetest nutriment to him,
His best Norwegian wines.

To satin races he is nought;
But children on the Don
Beneath his tabernacles play,
And Dnieper wrestlers run.

82

THERE's a certain slant of light
On winter afternoons,
That oppresses, like the weight
Of cathedral tunes.

Heavenly hurt it gives us;
We can find no scar,
But internal difference
Where the meanings are.

None may teach it anything,
'Tis the seal, despair,—
An imperial affliction
Sent us of the air.

When it comes, the landscape listens,
Shadows hold their breath;
When it goes, 'tis like the distance
On the look of death.

83

It will be Summer eventually—
Ladies with parasols,
Sauntering gentlemen with canes,
And little girls with dolls

Will tint the pallid landscape
As 'twere a bright bouquet,
Though drifted deep in Parian
The village lies to-day.

The lilacs, bending many a year,
Will sway with purple load;
The bees will not despise the tune
Their forefathers have hummed;

The wild rose redden in the bog,
The aster on the hill

Her everlasting fashion set,
And covenant gentians frill,

Till summer folds her miracle
As women do their gown,
Or priests adjust the symbols
When sacrament is done.

84

A LIGHT exists in spring
   Not present on the year
At any other period.
   When March is scarcely here

A color stands abroad
   On solitary hills
That science cannot overtake,
   But human nature *feels*.

It waits upon the lawn;
   It shows the furthest tree
Upon the furthest slope we know;
   It almost speaks to me.

Then, as horizons step,
   Or noons report away,
Without the formula of sound,
   It passes, and we stay:

A quality of loss
   Affecting our content,

As trade had suddenly encroached
    Upon a sacrament.

85

A LADY red upon the hill
    Her annual secret keeps;
A lady white within the field
    In placid lily sleeps!

The tidy breezes with their brooms
    Sweep vale, and hill, and tree!
Prithee, my pretty housewives!
    Who may expected be?

The neighbors do not yet suspect!
    The woods exchange a smile—
Orchard, and buttercup, and bird—
    In such a little while!

And yet how still the landscape stands,
    How nonchalant the wood,
As if the resurrection
    Were nothing very odd!

86

DEAR March, come in!
How glad I am!
I looked for you before.
Put down your hat—
You must have walked—

[116]

How out of breath you are!
Dear March, how are you?
And the rest?
Did you leave Nature well?
Oh, March, come right upstairs with me,
I have so much to tell!

I got your letter, and the bird's;
The maples never knew
That you were coming,—I declare,
How red their faces grew!
But, March, forgive me—
And all those hills
You left for me to hue;
There was no purple suitable,
You took it all with you.

Who knocks? That April!
Lock the door!
I will not be pursued!
He stayed away a year, to call
When I am occupied.
But trifles look so trivial
As soon as you have come,
That blame is just as dear as praise
And praise as mere as blame.

87

Not knowing when the dawn will come
    I open every door;
Or has it feathers like a bird,
    Or billows like a shore?

A murmur in the trees to note,
   Not loud enough for wind;
A star not far enough to seek,
   Nor near enough to find;

A long, long yellow on the lawn,
   A hubbub as of feet;
Not audible, as ours to us,
   But dapper, more sweet;

A hurrying home of little men
   To houses unperceived,—
All this, and more, if I should tell,
   Would never be believed.

Of robins in the trundle bed
   How many I espy
Whose nightgowns could not hide the wings,
   Although I heard them try!

But then I promised ne'er to tell;
   How could I break my word?
So go your way and I'll go mine,—
   No fear you'll miss the road.

*T*o my quick ear the leaves conferred;
   The bushes they were bells;
I could not find a privacy
   From Nature's sentinels.

In cave if I presumed to hide,
    The walls began to tell;
Creation seemed a mighty crack
    To make me visible.

90

High from the earth I heard a bird;
    He trod upon the trees
As he esteemed them trifles,
    And then he spied a breeze,
And situated softly
    Upon a pile of wind
Which in a perturbation
    Nature had left behind.
A joyous-going fellow
    I gathered from his talk,
Which both of benediction
    And badinage partook,
Without apparent burden,
    I learned, in leafy wood
He was the faithful father
    Of a dependent brood;
And this untoward transport
    His remedy for care,—
A contrast to our respites.
    How different we are!

91

The spider as an artist
    Has never been employed

Though his surpassing merit
    Is freely certified

By every broom and Bridget
    Throughout a Christian land.
Neglected son of genius,
    I take thee by the hand.

92

WHAT mystery pervades a well!
    The water lives so far,
Like neighbor from another world
    Residing in a jar.

The grass does not appear afraid;
    I often wonder he
Can stand so close and look so bold
    At what is dread to me.

Related somehow they may be,—
    The sedge stands next the sea,
Where he is floorless, yet of fear
    No evidence gives he.

But nature is a stranger yet;
    The ones that cite her most
Have never passed her haunted house,
    Nor simplified her ghost.

To pity those that know her not
    Is helped by the regret

That those who know her, know her less
   The nearer her they get.

93

To make a prairie it takes a clover and one bee,—
And revery.
The revery alone will do
If bees are few.

94

It's like the light,—
   A fashionless delight,
It's like the bee,—
   A dateless melody.

It's like the woods,
   Private like breeze,
Phraseless, yet it stirs
   The proudest trees.

It's like the morning,—
   Best when it's done,—
The everlasting clocks
   Chime noon.

95

Sweet is the swamp with its secrets,
   Until we meet a snake;
'Tis then we sigh for houses,
   And our departure take

At that enthralling gallop
   That only childhood knows.
A snake is summer's treason,
   And guile is where it goes.

96

Could I but ride indefinite,
   As doth the meadow-bee,
And visit only where I liked,
   And no man visit me,

And flirt all day with buttercups,
   And marry whom I may,
And dwell a little everywhere,
   Or better, run away

With no police to follow,
   Or chase me if I do,
Till I should jump peninsulas
   To get away from you,—

I said, but just to be a bee
   Upon a raft of air,
And row in nowhere all day long,
   And anchor off the bar,—
What liberty! So captives deem
   Who tight in dungeons are.

97

The moon was but a chin of gold
   A night or two ago,

And now she turns her perfect face
   Upon the world below.

Her forehead is of amplest blond;
   Her cheek like beryl stone;
Her eye unto the summer dew
   The likest I have known.

Her lips of amber never part;
   But what must be the smile
Upon her friend she could bestow
   Were such her silver will!

And what a privilege to be
   But the remotest star!
For certainly her way might pass
   Beside your twinkling door.

Her bonnet is the firmament,
   The universe her shoe,
The stars the trinkets at her belt,
   Her dimities of blue.

98

THE bat is dun with wrinkled wings
   Like fallow article,
And not a song pervades his lips,
   Or none perceptible.

His small umbrella, quaintly halved,
   Describing in the air

An arc alike inscrutable,—
    Elate philosopher!

Deputed from what firmament
    Of what astute abode,
Empowered with what malevolence
    Auspiciously withheld.

To his adroit Creator
    Ascribe no less the praise;
Beneficent, believe me,
    His eccentricities.

99

You've seen balloons set, haven't you?
    So stately they ascend
It is as swans discarded you
    For duties diamond.

Their liquid feet go softly out
    Upon a sea of blond;
They spurn the air as 'twere too mean
    For creatures so renowned.

Their ribbons just beyond the eye,
    They struggle some for breath,
And yet the crowd applauds below;
    They would not encore death.

The gilded creature strains and spins,
    Trips frantic in a tree,

Tears open her imperial veins
　　And tumbles in the sea.

The crowd retire with an oath,
　　The dust in streets goes down,
And clerks in counting-rooms observe,
　　" 'Twas only a balloon."

100

THE cricket sang,
　　And set the sun,
And workmen finished, one by one,
　　Their seam the day upon.

The low grass loaded with the dew,
The twilight stood as strangers do
With hat in hand, polite and new,
　　To stay as if, or go.

A vastness, as a neighbor, came,—
A wisdom without face or name,
A peace, as hemispheres at home,—
　　And so the night became.

101

DRAB habitation of whom?
Tabernacle or tomb,
Or dome of worm,
Or porch of gnome,
Or some elf's catacomb?

(Sent with a cocoon to her little nephew.)

[125]

OF bronze and blaze
    The north, to-night!
So adequate its forms,
So preconcerted with itself,
    So distant to alarms,—
An unconcern so sovereign
    To universe, or me,
It paints my simple spirit
    With tints of majesty,
Till I take vaster attitudes,
    And strut upon my stem,
Disdaining men and oxygen,
    For arrogance of them.

My splendors are menagerie;
    But their completeless show
Will entertain the centuries
    When I am, long ago,
An island in dishonored grass,
    Whom none but daisies know.

How the old mountains drip with sunset,
    And the brake of dun!
How the hemlocks are tipped in tinsel
    By the wizard sun!

How the old steeples hand the scarlet,
    Till the ball is full,—
Have I the lip of the flamingo
    That I dare to tell?

Then, how the fire ebbs like billows,
    Touching all the grass
With a departing, sapphire feature,
    As if a duchess pass!

How a small dusk crawls on the village
    Till the houses blot;
And the odd flambeaux no men carry
    Glimmer on the spot!

Now it is night in nest and kennel,
    And where was the wood,
Just a dome of abyss is nodding
    Into solitude!—

These are the visions baffled Guido;
    Titian never told;
Domenichino dropped the pencil,
    Powerless to unfold.

104

THE murmuring of bees has ceased;
    But murmuring of some
Posterior, prophetic,
    Has simultaneous come,—
The lower metres of the year,
    When nature's laugh is done,—
The Revelations of the book
    Whose Genesis is June.

PART THREE

LOVE

It's all I have to bring to-day,
  This, and my heart beside,
This, and my heart, and all the fields,
  And all the meadows wide.
Be sure you count, should I forget,—
  Some one the sum could tell,—
This, and my heart, and all the bees
  Which in the clover dwell.

1

$\mathcal{M}$ine by the right of the white election!
Mine by the royal seal!
Mine by the sign in the scarlet prison
Bars cannot conceal!

Mine, here in vision and in veto!
Mine, by the grave's repeal
Titled, confirmed,—delirious charter!
Mine, while the ages steal!

2

$\mathcal{Y}$ou left me, sweet, two legacies,—
A legacy of love
A Heavenly Father would content,
Had He the offer of;

You left me boundaries of pain
Capacious as the sea,
Between eternity and time,
Your consciousness and me.

3

$\mathcal{A}$lter? When the hills do.
Falter? When the sun
Question if his glory
Be the perfect one.

Surfeit? When the daffodil
Doth of the dew:

Even as herself, O friend!
I will of you!

4

ELYSIUM is as far as to
The very nearest room,
If in that room a friend await
Felicity or doom.

What fortitude the soul contains,
That it can so endure
The accent of a coming foot,
The opening of a door!

5

DOUBT me, my dim companion!
Why, God would be content
With but a fraction of the love
Poured thee without a stint.
The whole of me, forever,
What more the woman can,—
Say quick, that I may dower thee
With last delight I own!

It cannot be my spirit,
For that was thine before;
I ceded all of dust I knew,—
What opulence the more
Had I, a humble maiden,
Whose farthest of degree
Was that she might

Some distant heaven,
Dwell timidly with thee!

6

If you were coming in the fall,
I'd brush the summer by
With half a smile and half a spurn,
As housewives do a fly.

If I could see you in a year,
I'd wind the months in balls,
And put them each in separate drawers,
Until their time befalls.

If only centuries delayed,
I'd count them on my hand,
Subtracting till my fingers dropped
Into Van Diemen's land.

If certain, when this life was out,
That yours and mine should be,
I'd toss it yonder like a rind,
And taste eternity.

But now, all ignorant of the length
Of time's uncertain wing,
It goads me, like the goblin bee,
That will not state its sting.

7

J HIDE myself within my flower,
That wearing on your breast,

[1 3 3]

You, unsuspecting, wear me too—
And angels know the rest.

I hide myself within my flower,
That, fading from your vase,
You, unsuspecting, feel for me
Almost a loneliness.

8

THAT I did always love,
I bring thee proof:
That till I loved
I did not love enough.

That I shall love alway,
I offer thee
That love is life,
And life hath immortality.

This, dost thou doubt, sweet?
Then have I
Nothing to show
But Calvary.

9

HAVE you got a brook in your little heart,
Where bashful flowers blow,
And blushing birds go down to drink,
And shadows tremble so?

And nobody knows, so still it flows,
That any brook is there;

[1 3 4]

And yet your little draught of life
Is daily drunken there.

Then look out for the little brook in March,
When the rivers overflow,
And the snows come hurrying from the hills,
And the bridges often go.

And later, in August it may be,
When the meadows parching lie,
Beware, lest this little brook of life
Some burning noon go dry!

10

As if some little Arctic flower,
Upon the polar hem,
Went wandering down the latitudes,
Until it puzzled came
To continents of summer,
To firmaments of sun,
To strange, bright crowds of flowers,
And birds of foreign tongue!
I say, as if this little flower
To Eden wandered in—
What then? Why, nothing, only
Your inference therefrom!

11

My river runs to thee:
Blue sea, wilt welcome me?

My river waits reply.
Oh sea, look graciously!

I'll fetch thee brooks
From spotted nooks,—

Say, sea,
Take me!

12

I CANNOT live with you,
It would be life,
And life is over there
Behind the shelf

The sexton keeps the key to,
Putting up
Our life, his porcelain,
Like a cup

Discarded of the housewife,
Quaint or broken;
A newer Sèvres pleases,
Old ones crack.

I could not die with you,
For one must wait
To shut the other's gaze down,—
You could not.

And I, could I stand by
And see you freeze,

Without my right of frost,
Death's privilege?

Nor could I rise with you,
Because your face
Would put out Jesus',
That new grace

Glow plain and foreign
On my homesick eye,
Except that you, than he
Shone closer by.

They'd judge us—how?
For you served Heaven, you know,
Or sought to;
I could not,

Because you saturated sight,
And I had no more eyes
For sordid excellence
As Paradise.

And were you lost, I would be,
Though my name
Rang loudest
On the heavenly fame.

And were you saved,
And I condemned to be
Where you were not,
That self were hell to me.

[137]

So we must keep apart,
You there, I here,
With just the door ajar
That oceans are,
And prayer,
And that pale sustenance,
Despair!

13

THERE came a day at summer's full
Entirely for me;
I thought that such were for the saints,
Where revelations be.

The sun, as common, went abroad,
The flowers, accustomed, blew.
As if no sail the solstice passed
That maketh all things new.

The time was scarce profaned by speech;
The symbol of a word
Was needless, as at sacrament
The wardrobe of our Lord.

Each was to each the sealéd church,
Permitted to commune this time,
Lest we too awkward show
At supper of the Lamb.

The hours slid fast, as hours will,
Clutched tight by greedy hands;

So faces on two decks look back,
Bound to opposing lands.

And so, when all the time had failed,
Without external sound,
Each bound the other's crucifix,
We gave no other bond.

Sufficient troth that we shall rise—
Deposed, at length, the grave—
To that new marriage, justified
Through Calvaries of Love!

14

I'M ceded, I've stopped being theirs;
The name they dropped upon my face
With water, in the country church,
Is finished using now,
And they can put it with my dolls,
My childhood, and the string of spools
I've finished threading too.

Baptized before without the choice,
But this time consciously, of grace
Unto supremest name,
Called to my full, the crescent dropped,
Existence's whole arc filled up
With one small diadem.

My second rank, too small the first,
Crowned, crowing on my father's breast,

A half unconscious queen;
But this time, adequate, erect,
With will to choose or to reject,
And I choose—just a throne.

15

'Twas a long parting, but the time
For interview had come;
Before the judgment-seat of God,
The last and second time

These fleshless lovers met,
A heaven in a gaze,
A heaven of heavens, the privilege
Of one another's eyes.

No lifetime set on them,
Apparelled as the new
Unborn, except they had beheld,
Born everlasting now.

Was bridal e'er like this?
A paradise, the host,
And cherubim and seraphim
The most familiar guest.

16

I'm wife; I've finished that,
That other state;
I'm Czar, I'm woman now:
It's safer so.

How odd the girl's life looks
Behind this soft eclipse!
I think that earth seems so
To those in heaven now.

This being comfort, then
That other kind was pain;
But why compare?
I'm wife! stop there!

17

SHE rose to his requirement, dropped
The playthings of her life
To take the honorable work
Of woman and of wife.

If aught she missed in her new day
Of amplitude, or awe,
Or first prospective, or the gold
In using wore away,

It lay unmentioned, as the sea
Develops pearl and weed,
But only to himself is known
The fathoms they abide.

18

COME slowly, Eden!
Lips unused to thee,
Bashful, sip thy jasmines,
As the fainting bee,

[141]

Reaching late his flower,
Round her chamber hums,
Counts his nectars—enters,
And is lost in balms!

19

Of all the souls that stand create
I have elected one.
When sense from spirit files away,
And subterfuge is done;

When that which is and that which was
Apart, intrinsic, stand,
And this brief tragedy of flesh
Is shifted like a sand;

When figures show their royal front
And mists are carved away,—
Behold the atom I preferred
To all the lists of clay!

20

I have no life but this,
To lead it here;
Nor any death, but lest
Dispelled from there;

Nor tie to earths to come,
Nor action new,
Except through this extent,
The realm of you.

21

Your riches taught me poverty.
Myself a millionaire
In little wealths,—as girls could boast,—
Till broad as Buenos Ayre,

You drifted your dominions
A different Peru;
And I esteemed all poverty,
For life's estate with you.

Of mines I little know, myself,
But just the names of gems,—
The colors of the commonest;
And scarce of diadems

So much that, did I meet the queen,
Her glory I should know:
But this must be a different wealth,
To miss it beggars so.

I'm sure 'tis India all day
To those who look on you
Without a stint, without a blame,—
Might I but be the Jew!

I'm sure it is Golconda,
Beyond my power to deem,—
To have a smile for mine each day,
How better than a gem!

At least, it solaces to know
That there exists a gold,

Although I prove it just in time
Its distance to behold!

It's far, far treasure to surmise,
And estimate the pearl
That slipped my simple fingers through
While just a girl at school!

22

I GAVE myself to him,
And took himself for pay.
The solemn contract of a life
Was ratified this way.

The wealth might disappoint,
Myself a poorer prove
Than this great purchaser suspect,
The daily own of Love

Depreciate the vision;
But, till the merchant buy,
Still fable, in the isles of spice,
The subtle cargoes lie.

At least, 'tis mutual risk,—
Some found it mutual gain;
Sweet debt of Life,—each night to owe,
Insolvent, every noon.

23

"GOING to him! Happy letter! Tell him—
Tell him the page I didn't write;

Tell him I only said the syntax,
And left the verb and the pronoun out.
Tell him just how the fingers hurried,
Then how they waded, slow, slow, slow;
And then you wished you had eyes in your pages,
So you could see what moved them so.

"Tell him it wasn't a practised writer,
You guessed, from the way the sentence toiled;
You could hear the bodice tug, behind you,
As if it held but the might of a child;
You almost pitied it, you, it worked so.
Tell him— No, you may quibble there,
For it would split his heart to know it,
And then you and I were silenter.

"Tell him night finished before we finished,
And the old clock kept neighing 'day!'
And you got sleepy and begged to be ended—
What could it hinder so, to say?
Tell him just how she sealed you, cautious,
But if he ask where you are hid
Until to-morrow,—happy letter!
Gesture, coquette, and shake your head!"

24

THE way I read a letter's this:
'Tis first I lock the door,
And push it with my fingers next,
For transport it be sure.

And then I go the furthest off
To counteract a knock;
Then draw my little letter forth
And softly pick its lock.

Then, glancing narrow at the wall,
And narrow at the floor,
For firm conviction of a mouse
Not exorcised before,

Peruse how infinite I am
To—no one that you know!
And sigh for lack of heaven,—but not
The heaven the creeds bestow.

25

*W*ILD nights! Wild nights!
Were I with thee,
Wild nights should be
Our luxury!

Futile the winds
To a heart in port,—
Done with the compass,
Done with the chart.

Rowing in Eden!
Ah! the sea!
Might I but moor
To-night in thee!

THE night was wide, and furnished scant
With but a single star,
That often as a cloud it met
Blew out itself for fear.

The wind pursued the little bush,
And drove away the leaves
November left; then clambered up
And fretted in the eaves.

No squirrel went abroad;
A dog's belated feet
Like intermittent plush were heard
Adown the empty street.

To feel if blinds be fast,
And closer to the fire
Her little rocking-chair to draw,
And shiver for the poor,

The housewife's gentle task.
"How pleasanter," said she
Unto the sofa opposite,
"The sleet than May—no thee!"

27

DID the harebell loose her girdle
To the lover bee,
Would the bee the harebell hallow
Much as formerly?

Did the paradise, persuaded,
Yield her moat of pearl,
Would the Eden be an Eden,
Or the earl an earl?

28

A CHARM invests a face
Imperfectly beheld,—
The lady dare not lift her veil
For fear it be dispelled.

But peers beyond her mesh,
And wishes, and denies,—
Lest interview annul a want
That image satisfies.

29

THE rose did caper on her cheek,
Her bodice rose and fell,
Her pretty speech, like drunken men,
Did stagger pitiful.

Her fingers fumbled at her work,—
Her needle would not go;
What ailed so smart a little maid
It puzzled me to know,

Till opposite I spied a cheek
That bore another rose;
Just opposite, another speech
That like the drunkard goes;

[148]

A vest that, like the bodice, danced
To the immortal tune,—
Till those two troubled little clocks
Ticked softly into one.

30

In lands I never saw, they say,
Immortal Alps look down,
Whose bonnets touch the firmament,
Whose sandals touch the town,—

Meek at whose everlasting feet
A myriad daisies play.
Which, sir, are you, and which am I,
Upon an August day?

31

The moon is distant from the sea,
And yet with amber hands
She leads him, docile as a boy,
Along appointed sands.

He never misses a degree;
Obedient to her eye,
He comes just so far toward the town,
Just so far goes away.

Oh, Signor, thine the amber hand,
And mine the distant sea,—
Obedient to the last command
Thine eyes impose on me.

32

HE put the belt around my life,—
I heard the buckle snap,
And turned away, imperial,
My lifetime folding up
Deliberate, as a duke would do
A kingdom's title-deed,—
Henceforth a dedicated sort,
A member of the cloud.

Yet not too far to come at call,
And do the little toils
That make the circuit of the rest,
And deal occasional smiles
To lives that stoop to notice mine
And kindly ask it in,—
Whose invitation, knew you not
For whom I must decline?

I HELD a jewel in my fingers
And went to sleep.
The day was warm, and winds were prosy
I said : " 'Twill keep."

I woke and chid my honest fingers,—
The gem was gone;
And now an amethyst remembrance
Is all I own.

WHAT if I say I shall not wait?
What if I burst the fleshly gate
And pass, escaped, to thee?
What if I file this mortal off,
See where it hurt me,—that's enough,—
And wade in liberty?

They cannot take us any more,—
Dungeons may call, and guns implore;
Unmeaning now, to me,
As laughter was an hour ago,
Or laces, or a travelling show,
Or who died yesterday!

PROUD of my broken heart since thou didst break it,
    Proud of the pain I did not feel till thee,
Proud of my night since thou with moons dost slake it,
    Not to partake thy passion, my humility.

MY worthiness is all my doubt,
    His merit all my fear,
Contrasting which, my qualities
    Do lowlier appear;

Lest I should insufficient prove
    For his beloved need,
The chiefest apprehension
    Within my loving creed.

So I, the undivine abode
    Of his elect content,
Conform my soul as 'twere a church
    Unto her sacrament.

37

Love is anterior to life,
    Posterior to death,
Initial of creation, and
    The exponent of breath.

38

One blessing had I, than the rest
    So larger to my eyes
That I stopped gauging, satisfied,
    For this enchanted size.

It was the limit of my dream,
    The focus of my prayer,—
A perfect, paralyzing bliss
    Contented as despair.

I knew no more of want or cold,
    Phantasms both become,
For this new value in the soul,
    Supremest earthly sum.

The heaven below the heaven above
    Obscured with ruddier hue.
Life's latitude leant over-full;
    The judgment perished, too.

Why joys so scantily disburse,
    Why Paradise defer,
Why floods are served to us in bowls,—
    I speculate no more.

39

WHEN roses cease to bloom, dear,
    And violets are done,
When bumble-bees in solemn flight
    Have passed beyond the sun,

The hand that paused to gather
    Upon this summer's day
Will idle lie, in Auburn,—
    Then take my flower, pray!

40

SUMMER for thee grant I may be
    When summer days are flown!
Thy music still when whippoorwill
    And oriole are done!

For thee to bloom, I'll skip the tomb
    And sow my blossoms o'er!
Pray gather me, Anemone,
    Thy flower forevermore!

41

SPLIT the lark and you'll find the music,
    Bulb after bulb, in silver rolled,

Scantily dealt to the summer morning,
    Saved for your ear when lutes be old.

Loose the flood, you shall find it patent,
    Gush after gush, reserved for you;
Scarlet experiment! sceptic Thomas,
    Now, do you doubt that your bird was true?

42

To lose thee, sweeter than to gain
    All other hearts I knew.
'Tis true the drought is destitute,
    But then I had the dew!

The Caspian has its realms of sand,
    Its other realm of sea;
Without the sterile perquisite
    No Caspian could be.

43

    Poor little heart!
    Did they forget thee?
Then dinna care! Then dinna care!

    Proud little heart!
    Did they forsake thee?
Be debonair! Be debonair!

    Frail little heart!
    I would not break thee:
Could'st credit me? Could'st credit me?

[154]

Gay little heart!
  Like morning glory
Thou'll wilted be; thou'll wilted be!

44

THERE is a word
    Which bears a sword
    Can pierce an armed man.
It hurls its barbed syllables,—
    At once is mute again.
But where it fell
The saved will tell
    On patriotic day,
Some epauletted brother
    Gave his breath away.

Wherever runs the breathless sun,
    Wherever roams the day,
There is its noiseless onset,
    There is its victory!
Behold the keenest marksman!
    The most accomplished shot!
Time's sublimest target
    Is a soul "forgot"!

45

HE fumbles at your spirit
    As players at the keys
Before they drop full music on;
    He stuns you by degrees,

Prepares your brittle substance
　For the ethereal blow,
By fainter hammers, further heard,
　Then nearer, then so slow

Your breath has time to straighten,
　Your brain to bubble cool,—
Deals one imperial thunderbolt
　That scalps your naked soul.

46

HEART, we will forget him!
　You and I, to-night!
You may forget the warmth he gave,
　I will forget the light.

When you have done, pray tell me,
　That I my thoughts may dim;
Haste! lest while you're lagging,
　I may remember him!

47

FATHER, I bring thee not myself,—
　That were the little load;
I bring thee the imperial heart
　I had not strength to hold.

The heart I cherished in my own
　Till mine too heavy grew,
Yet strangest, heavier since it went,
　Is it too large for you?

[1 5 6]

WE outgrow love like other things
    And put it in the drawer,
Till it an antique fashion shows
    Like costumes grandsires wore.

NOT with a club the heart is broken,
    Nor with a stone;
A whip, so small you could not see it,
    I've known
To lash the magic creature
    Till it fell,
Yet that whip's name too noble
    Then to tell.

Magnanimous of bird
    By boy descried,
To sing unto the stone
    Of which it died.

MY friend must be a bird,
    Because it flies!
Mortal my friend must be,
    Because it dies!
Barbs has it, like a bee.
Ah, curious friend,
    Thou puzzlest me!

HE touched me, so I live to know
    That such a day, permitted so,
  I groped upon his breast.
It was a boundless place to me,
And silenced, as the awful sea
  Puts minor streams to rest.

And now, I'm different from before,
As if I breathed superior air,
  Or brushed a royal gown;
My feet, too, that had wandered so,
My gypsy face transfigured now
  To tenderer renown.

LET me not mar that perfect dream
  By an auroral stain,
But so adjust my daily night
  That it will come again.

I LIVE with him, I see his face;
  I go no more away
For visitor, or sundown;
  Death's single privacy,

The only one forestalling mine,
  And that by right that he
Presents a claim invisible,
  No wedlock granted me.

I live with him, I hear his voice,
    I stand alive to-day
To witness to the certainty
    Of immortality

Taught me by Time,—the lower way,
    Conviction every day,—
That life like this is endless,
    Be judgment what it may.

54

J ENVY seas whereon he rides,
    I envy spokes of wheels
Of chariots that him convey,
    I envy speechless hills

That gaze upon his journey;
    How easy all can see
What is forbidden utterly
    As heaven, unto me!

I envy nests of sparrows
    That dot his distant eaves,
The wealthy fly upon his pane,
    The happy, happy leaves

That just abroad his window
    Have summer's leave to be,
The earrings of Pizarro
    Could not obtain for me.

I envy light that wakes him,
    And bells that boldly ring

To tell him it is noon abroad,—
  Myself his noon could bring,

Yet interdict my blossom
  And abrogate my bee,
Lest noon in everlasting night
  Drop Gabriel and me.

55

A SOLEMN thing it was, I said,
  A woman white to be,
And wear, if God should count me fit
  Her hallowed mystery.

A timid thing to drop a life
  Into the purple well,
Too plummetless that it come back
  Eternity until.

PART FOUR

TIME AND ETERNITY

1

ONE dignity delays for all,
One mitred afternoon.
None can avoid this purple,
None evade this crown.

Coach it insures, and footmen,
Chamber and state and throng;
Bells, also, in the village,
As we ride grand along.

What dignified attendants,
What service when we pause!
How loyally at parting
Their hundred hats they raise!

How pomp surpassing ermine,
When simple you and I
Present our meek escutcheon,
And claim the rank to die!

2

DELAYED till she had ceased to know,
 Delayed till in its vest of snow
 Her loving bosom lay.
An hour behind the fleeting breath,
Later by just an hour than death,—
 Oh, lagging yesterday!

Could she have guessed that it would be;
Could but a crier of the glee
 Have climbed the distant hill;

[163]

Had not the bliss so slow a pace,—
Who knows but this surrendered face
　　Were undefeated still?

Oh, if there may departing be
Any forgot by victory
　　In her imperial round,
Show them this meek apparelled thing,
That could not stop to be a king,
　　Doubtful if it be crowned!

3

DEPARTED to the judgment,
A mighty afternoon;
Great clouds like ushers leaning,
Creation looking on.

The flesh surrendered, cancelled,
The bodiless begun;
Two worlds, like audiences, disperse
And leave the soul alone.

4

SAFE in their alabaster chambers,
Untouched by morning and untouched by noon,
Sleep the meek members of the resurrection,
Rafter of satin, and roof of stone.

Light laughs the breeze in her castle of sunshine;
Babbles the bee in a stolid ear;
Pipe the sweet birds in ignorant cadence,—
Ah, what sagacity perished here!

Grand go the years in the crescent above them;
Worlds scoop their arcs, and firmaments row,
Diadems drop and Doges surrender,
Soundless as dots on a disk of snow.

5

On this long storm the rainbow rose,
On this late morn the sun;
The clouds, like listless elephants,
Horizons straggled down.

The birds rose smiling in their nests,
The gales indeed were done;
Alas! how heedless were the eyes
On whom the summer shone!

The quiet nonchalance of death
No daybreak can bestir;
The slow archangel's syllables
Must awaken her.

6

My cocoon tightens, colors tease,
I'm feeling for the air;
A dim capacity for wings
Degrades the dress I wear.

A power of butterfly must be
The aptitude to fly,
Meadows of majesty concedes
And easy sweeps of sky.

[165]

So I must baffle at the hint
And cipher at the sign,
And make much blunder, if at last
I take the clew divine.

7

EXULTATION is the going
Of an inland soul to sea,—
Past the houses, past the headlands,
Into deep eternity!

Bred as we, among the mountains,
Can the sailor understand
The divine intoxication
Of the first league out from land?

8

LOOK back on time with kindly eyes,
He doubtless did his best;
How softly sinks his trembling sun
In human nature's west!

9

A TRAIN went through a burial gate,
A bird broke forth and sang,
And trilled, and quivered, and shook his throat
Till all the churchyard rang;

And then adjusted his little notes,
And bowed and sang again.

Doubtless, he thought it meet of him
To say good-by to men.

10

J DIED for beauty, but was scarce
Adjusted in the tomb,
When one who died for truth was lain
In an adjoining room.

He questioned softly why I failed?
"For beauty," I replied.
"And I for truth,—the two are one;
We brethren are," he said.

And so, as kinsmen met a night,
We talked between the rooms,
Until the moss had reached our lips,
And covered up our names.

11

How many times these low feet staggered,
Only the soldered mouth can tell;
Try! can you stir the awful rivet?
Try! can you lift the hasps of steel?

Stroke the cool forehead, hot so often,
Lift, if you can, the listless hair;
Handle the adamantine fingers
Never a thimble more shall wear.

Buzz the dull flies on the chamber window;
Brave shines the sun through the freckled pane;

Fearless the cobweb swings from the ceiling—
Indolent housewife, in daisies lain!

12

I LIKE a look of agony,
Because I know it's true;
Men do not sham convulsion,
Nor simulate a throe.

The eyes glaze once, and that is death.
Impossible to feign
The beads upon the forehead
By homely anguish strung.

13

THAT short, potential stir
That each can make but once,
That bustle so illustrious
'Tis almost consequence,

Is the *éclat* of death.
Oh, thou unknown renown
That not a beggar would accept,
Had he the power to spurn!

14

I WENT to thank her,
But she slept;
Her bed a funnelled stone,
With nosegays at the head and foot,
That travellers had thrown,

Who went to thank her;
But she slept.
'Twas short to cross the sea
To look upon her like, alive,
But turning back 'twas slow.

15

I'VE seen a dying eye
Run round and round a room
In search of something, as it seemed,
Then cloudier become;
And then, obscure with fog,
And then be soldered down,
Without disclosing what it be,
'Twere blessed to have seen.

16

THE clouds their backs together laid,
The north begun to push,
The forests galloped till they fell,
The lightning skipped like mice;
The thunder crumbled like a stuff—
How good to be safe in tombs,
Where nature's temper cannot reach,
Nor vengeance ever comes!

17

I NEVER saw a moor,
I never saw the sea;

Yet know I how the heather looks,
And what a wave must be.

I never spoke with God,
Nor visited in heaven;
Yet certain am I of the spot
As if the chart were given.

18

God permits industrious angels
Afternoons to play.
I met one,—forgot my school-mates,
All, for him, straightway.

God calls home the angels promptly
At the setting sun;
I missed mine. How dreary marbles,
After playing Crown!

19

To know just how he suffered would be dear;
To know if any human eyes were near
To whom he could intrust his wavering gaze,
Until it settled firm on Paradise.

To know if he was patient, part content,
Was dying as he thought, or different;
Was it a pleasant day to die,
And did the sunshine face his way?

What was his furthest mind, of home, or God,
Or what the distant say

At news that he ceased human nature
On such a day?

And wishes, had he any?
Just his sigh, accented,
Had been legible to me.
And was he confident until
Ill fluttered out in everlasting well?

And if he spoke, what name was best,
What first,
What one broke off with
At the drowsiest?

Was he afraid, or tranquil?
Might he know
How conscious consciousness could grow,
Till love that was, and love too blest to be,
Meet—and the junction be Eternity?

20

THE last night that she lived,
It was a common night,
Except the dying; this to us
Made nature different.

We noticed smallest things,—
Things overlooked before,
By this great light upon our minds
Italicized, as 'twere.

That others could exist
While she must finish quite,

A jealousy for her arose
So nearly infinite.

We waited while she passed;
It was a narrow time,
Too jostled were our souls to speak,
At length the notice came.

She mentioned, and forgot;
Then lightly as a reed
Bent to the water, shivered scarce,
Consented, and was dead.

And we, we placed the hair,
And drew the head erect;
And then an awful leisure was,
Our faith to regulate.

21

Not in this world to see his face
Sounds long, until I read the place
Where this is said to be
But just the primer to a life
Unopened, rare, upon the shelf,
Clasped yet to him and me.

And yet, my primer suits me so
I would not choose a book to know
Than that, be sweeter wise;
Might some one else so learned be,
And leave me just my A B C,
Himself could have the skies.

*T*HE bustle in a house
The morning after death
Is solemnest of industries
Enacted upon earth,—

The sweeping up the heart,
And putting love away
We shall not want to use again
Until eternity.

I REASON, earth is short,
And anguish absolute,
And many hurt;
But what of that?

I reason, we could die:
The best vitality
Cannot excel decay;
But what of that?

I reason that in heaven
Somehow, it will be even,
Some new equation given;
But what of that?

*A*FRAID? Of whom am I afraid?
Not death; for who is he?

The porter of my father's lodge
As much abasheth me.

Of life? 'Twere odd I fear a thing
That comprehendeth me
In one or more existences
At Deity's decree.

Of resurrection? Is the east
Afraid to trust the morn
With her fastidious forehead?
As soon impeach my crown!

25

THE sun kept setting, setting still;
No hue of afternoon
Upon the village I perceived,—
From house to house 'twas noon.

The dusk kept dropping, dropping still;
No dew upon the grass,
But only on my forehead stopped,
And wandered in my face.

My feet kept drowsing, drowsing still,
My fingers were awake;
Yet why so little sound myself
Unto my seeming make?

How well I knew the light before!
I could not see it now.

'Tis dying, I am doing; but
I'm not afraid to know.

26

Two swimmers wrestled on the spar
Until the morning sun,
When one turned smiling to the land.
O God, the other one!

The stray ships passing spied a face
Upon the waters borne,
With eyes in death still begging raised,
And hands beseeching thrown.

27

BECAUSE I could not stop for Death,
He kindly stopped for me;
The carriage held but just ourselves
And Immortality.

We slowly drove, he knew no haste,
And I had put away
My labor, and my leisure too,
For his civility.

We passed the school where children played
At wrestling in a ring;
We passed the fields of gazing grain,
We passed the setting sun.

We paused before a house that seemed
A swelling of the ground;

The roof was scarcely visible,
The cornice but a mound.

Since then 'tis centuries; but each
Feels shorter than the day
I first surmised the horses' heads
Were toward eternity.

28

SHE went as quiet as the dew
From a familiar flower.
Not like the dew did she return
At the accustomed hour!

She dropt as softly as a star
From out my summer's eve;
Less skillful than Leverrier
It's sorer to believe!

29

AT last to be identified!
At last, the lamps upon thy side,
The rest of life to see!
Past midnight, past the morning star!
Past sunrise! Ah! what leagues there are
Between our feet and day!

30

EXCEPT to heaven, she is nought;
Except for angels, lone;

[176]

Except to some wide-wandering bee,
A flower superfluous blown;

Except for winds, provincial;
Except by butterflies,
Unnoticed as a single dew
That on the acre lies.

The smallest housewife in the grass,
Yet take her from the lawn,
And somebody has lost the face
That made existence home!

31

DEATH is a dialogue between
The spirit and the dust.
"Dissolve," says Death. The Spirit, "Sir,
I have another trust."

Death doubts it, argues from the ground.
The Spirit turns away,
Just laying off, for evidence,
An overcoat of clay.

32

IT was too late for man,
But early yet for God;
Creation impotent to help,
But prayer remained our side.

How excellent the heaven,
When earth cannot be had;

How hospitable, then, the face
Of our old neighbor, God!

33

WHEN I was small, a woman died.
To-day her only boy
Went up from the Potomac,
His face all victory,

To look at her; how slowly
The seasons must have turned
Till bullets clipt an angle,
And he passed quickly round!

If pride shall be in Paradise
I never can decide;
Of their imperial conduct,
No person testified.

But proud in apparition,
That woman and her boy
Pass back and forth before my brain,
As ever in the sky.

34

THE daisy follows soft the sun,
     And when his golden walk is done,
   Sits shyly at his feet.
He, waking, finds the flower near.
"Wherefore, marauder, art thou here?"
   "Because, sir, love is sweet!"

We are the flower, Thou the sun!
Forgive us, if as days decline,
    We nearer steal to Thee,—
Enamoured of the parting west,
The peace, the flight, the amethyst,
    Night's possibility!

35

No rack can torture me,
My soul's at liberty.
Behind this mortal bone
There knits a bolder one

You cannot prick with saw,
Nor rend with scimitar.
Two bodies therefore be;
Bind one, and one will flee.

The eagle of his nest
No easier divest
And gain the sky,
Than mayest thou,

Except thyself may be
Thine enemy;
Captivity is consciousness,
So's liberty.

36

I LOST a world the other day.
Has anybody found?

[179]

You'll know it by the row of stars
Around its forehead bound.

A rich man might not notice it;
Yet to my frugal eye
Of more esteem than ducats.
Oh, find it, sir, for me!

37

IF I shouldn't be alive
When the robins come,
Give the one in red cravat
A memorial crumb.

If I couldn't thank you,
Being just asleep,
You will know I'm trying
With my granite lip!

38

SLEEP is supposed to be,
By souls of sanity,
The shutting of the eye.

Sleep is the station grand
Down which on either hand
The hosts of witness stand!

Morn is supposed to be,
By people of degree,
The breaking of the day.

Morning has not occurred!
That shall aurora be
East of eternity;

One with the banner gay,
One in the red array,—
That is the break of day.

I SHALL know why, when time is over,
And I have ceased to wonder why;
Christ will explain each separate anguish
In the fair schoolroom of the sky.

He will tell me what Peter promised,
And I, for wonder at his woe,
I shall forget the drop of anguish
That scalds me now, that scalds me now.

I NEVER lost as much but twice,
And that was in the sod;
Twice have I stood a beggar
Before the door of God!

Angels, twice descending,
Reimbursed my store.
Burglar, banker, father,
I am poor once more!

LET down the bars, O Death!
The tired flocks come in
Whose bleating ceases to repeat,
Whose wandering is done.

Thine is the stillest night,
Thine the securest fold;
Too near thou art for seeking thee,
Too tender to be told.

GOING to heaven!
I don't know when,
Pray do not ask me how,—
Indeed, I'm too astonished
To think of answering you!
Going to heaven!—
How dim it sounds!
And yet it will be done
As sure as flocks go home at night
Unto the shepherd's arm!

Perhaps you're going too!
Who knows?
If you should get there first,
Save just a little place for me
Close to the two I lost!
The smallest "robe" will fit me,
And just a bit of "crown";

For you know we do not mind our dress
When we are going home.

I'm glad I don't believe it,
For it would stop my breath,
And I'd like to look a little more
At such a curious earth!
I am glad they did believe it
Whom I have never found
Since the mighty autumn afternoon
I left them in the ground.

43

At least to pray is left, is left.
O Jesus! in the air
I know not which thy chamber is,—
I'm knocking everywhere.

Thou stirrest earthquake in the South,
And maelstrom in the sea;
Say, Jesus Christ of Nazareth,
Hast thou no arm for me?

44

Step lightly on this narrow spot!
The broadest land that grows
Be not so ample as the breast
These emerald seams enclose.

Step lofty; for this name is told
As far as cannon dwell,

Or flag subsist, or fame export
Her deathless syllable.

45

Morns like these we parted;
Noons like these she rose,
Fluttering first, then firmer,
To her fair repose.

Never did she lisp it,
And 'twas not for me;
She was mute from transport,
I, from agony!

Till the evening, nearing,
One the shutters drew—
Quick! a sharper rustling!
And this linnet flew!

46

A DEATH-BLOW is a life-blow to some
Who, till they died, did not alive become;
Who, had they lived, had died, but when
They died, vitality begun.

47

I READ my sentence steadily,
Reviewed it with my eyes,
To see that I made no mistake
In its extremest clause,—

The date, and manner of the shame;
And then the pious form
That "God have mercy" on the soul
The jury voted him.

I made my soul familiar
With her extremity,
That at the last it should not be
A novel agony,

But she and Death, acquainted,
Meet tranquilly as friends,
Salute and pass without a hint—
And there the matter ends.

48

I HAVE not told my garden yet,
Lest that should conquer me;
I have not quite the strength now
To break it to the bee.

I will not name it in the street,
For shops would stare, that I,
So shy, so very ignorant,
Should have the face to die.

The hillsides must not know it,
Where I have rambled so,
Nor tell the loving forests
The day that I shall go,

Nor lisp it at the table,
Nor heedless by the way

Hint that within the riddle
One will walk to-day!

49

*T*HEY dropped like flakes, they dropped like stars,
   Like petals from a rose,
When suddenly across the June
   A wind with fingers goes.

They perished in the seamless grass,—
   No eye could find the place;
But God on his repealless list
   Can summon every face.

50

*T*HE only ghost I ever saw
Was dressed in mechlin,—so;
He wore no sandal on his foot,
And stepped like flakes of snow.
His gait was soundless, like the bird,
But rapid, like the roe;
His fashions quaint, mosaic,
Or, haply, mistletoe.

His conversation seldom,
His laughter like the breeze
That dies away in dimples
Among the pensive trees.
Our interview was transient,—
Of me, himself was shy;

And God forbid I look behind
Since that appalling day!

51

Some, too fragile for winter winds,
The thoughtful grave encloses,—
Tenderly tucking them in from frost
Before their feet are cold.

Never the treasures in her nest
The cautious grave exposes,
Building where schoolboy dare not look
And sportsman is not bold.

This covert have all the children
Early aged, and often cold,—
Sparrows unnoticed by the Father;
Lambs for whom time had not a fold.

52

As by the dead we love to sit,
Become so wondrous dear,
As for the lost we grapple,
Though all the rest are here,—

In broken mathematics
We estimate our prize,
Vast, in its fading ratio,
To our penurious eyes!

[187]

53

DEATH sets a thing significant
The eye had hurried by,
Except a perished creature
Entreat us tenderly

To ponder little workmanships
In crayon or in wool,
With "This was last her fingers did,"
Industrious until

The thimble weighed too heavy,
The stitches stopped themselves,
And then 'twas put among the dust
Upon the closet shelves.

A book I have, a friend gave,
Whose pencil, here and there,
Had notched the place that pleased him,—
At rest his fingers are.

Now, when I read, I read not,
For interrupting tears
Obliterate the etchings
Too costly for repairs.

54

I WENT to heaven,—
'Twas a small town,
Lit with a ruby,
Lathed with down.

[188]

Stiller than the fields
At the full dew,
Beautiful as pictures
No man drew.
People like the moth,
Of mechlin frames,
Duties of gossamer,
And eider names.
Almost contented
I could be
'Mong such unique
Society.

55

THEIR height in heaven comforts not,
Their glory nought to me;
'Twas best imperfect, as it was;
I'm finite, I can't see.

The house of supposition,
The glimmering frontier
That skirts the acres of perhaps,
To me shows insecure.

The wealth I had contented me;
If 'twas a meaner size,
Then I had counted it until
It pleased my narrow eyes

Better than larger values,
However true their show;

This timid life of evidence
Keeps pleading, "I don't know."

56

THERE is a shame of nobleness
Confronting sudden pelf,—
A finer shame of ecstasy
Convicted of itself.

A best disgrace a brave man feels,
Acknowledged of the brave,—
One more "Ye Blessed" to be told;
But this involves the grave.

57

TRIUMPH may be of several kinds.
There's triumph in the room
When that old imperator, Death,
By faith is overcome.

There's triumph of the finer mind
When truth, affronted long,
Advances calm to her supreme,
Her God her only throng.

A triumph when temptation's bribe
Is slowly handed back,
One eye upon the heaven renounced
And one upon the rack.

Severer triumph, by himself
Experienced, who can pass

Acquitted from that naked bar,
Jehovah's countenance!

58

POMPLESS no life can pass away;
    The lowliest career
To the same pageant wends its way
    As that exalted here.

How cordial is the mystery!
    The hospitable pall
A "this way" beckons spaciously,—
    A miracle for all!

59

J NOTICED people disappeared,
When but a little child,—
Supposed they visited remote,
Or settled regions wild.

Now know I they both visited
And settled regions wild,
But did because they died,—a fact
Withheld the little child!

60

J HAD no cause to be awake,
My best was gone to sleep,
And morn a new politeness took
And failed to wake them up,

But called the others clear,
And passed their curtains by.
Sweet morning, when I over-sleep,
Knock, recollect, for me!

I looked at sunrise once,
And then I looked at them,
And wishfulness in me arose
For circumstance the same.

'Twas such an ample peace,
It could not hold a sigh,—
'Twas Sabbath with the bells divorced,
'Twas sunset all the day.

So choosing but a gown
And taking but a prayer,
The only raiment I should need,
I struggled, and was there.

61

If anybody's friend be dead,
It's sharpest of the theme
The thinking how they walked alive,
At such and such a time.

Their costume, of a Sunday,
Some manner of the hair,—
A prank nobody knew but them,
Lost, in the sepulchre.

How warm they were on such a day:
You almost feel the date,
So short way off it seems; and now,
They're centuries from that.

How pleased they were at what you said;
You try to touch the smile,
And dip your fingers in the frost:
When was it, can you tell,

You asked the company to tea,
Acquaintance, just a few,
And chatted close with this grand thing
That don't remember you?

Past bows and invitations,
Past interview, and vow,
Past what ourselves can estimate,—
That makes the quick of woe!

62

Our journey had advanced;
Our feet were almost come
To that odd fork in Being's road,
Eternity by term.

Our pace took sudden awe,
Our feet reluctant led.
Before were cities, but between,
The forest of the dead.

Retreat was out of hope,—
Behind, a sealéd route,

Eternity's white flag before,
And God at every gate.

63

*A*MPLE make this bed.
Make this bed with awe;
In it wait till judgment break
Excellent and fair.

Be its mattress straight,
Be its pillow round;
Let no sunrise' yellow noise
Interrupt this ground.

64

O*N* such a night, or such a night,
Would anybody care
If such a little figure
Slipped quiet from its chair,

So quiet, oh, how quiet!
That nobody might know
But that the little figure
Rocked softer, to and fro?

On such a dawn, or such a dawn,
Would anybody sigh
That such a little figure
Too sound asleep did lie

For chanticleer to wake it,—
Or stirring house below,

Or giddy bird in orchard,
Or early task to do?

There was a little figure plump
For every little knoll,
Busy needles, and spools of thread,
And trudging feet from school.

Playmates, and holidays, and nuts,
And visions vast and small.
Strange that the feet so precious charged
Should reach so small a goal!

65

ESSENTIAL oils are wrung:
The attar from the rose
Is not expressed by suns alone,
It is the gift of screws.

The general rose decays;
But this, in lady's drawer,
Makes summer when the lady lies
In ceaseless rosemary.

66

I LIVED on dread; to those who know
The stimulus there is
In danger, other impetus
Is numb and vital-less.

As 'twere a spur upon the soul,
A fear will urge it where

[195]

To go without the spectre's **aid**
Were challenging despair.

67

If I should die,
And you should live,
And time should gurgle on,
And morn should beam,
And noon should burn,
As it has usual done;
If birds should build as early,
And bees as bustling go,—
One might depart at option
From enterprise below!
'Tis sweet to know that stocks will **stand**
When we with daisies lie,
That commerce will continue,
And trades as briskly fly.
It makes the parting tranquil
And keeps the soul serene,
That gentlemen so sprightly
Conduct the pleasing scene!

68

Her final summer was it,
And yet we guessed it not;
If tenderer industriousness
Pervaded her, we thought

A further force of life
Developed from within,—

When Death lit all the shortness up,
And made the hurry plain.

We wondered at our blindness,—
When nothing was to see
But her Carrara guide-post,—
At our stupidity,

When, duller than our dulness,
The busy darling lay,
So busy was she, finishing,
So leisurely were we!

69

ONE need not be a chamber to be haunted,
One need not be a house;
The brain has corridors surpassing
Material place.

Far safer, of a midnight meeting
External ghost,
Than an interior confronting
That whiter host.

Far safer through an Abbey gallop,
The stones achase,
Than, moonless, one's own self encounter
In lonesome place.

Ourself, behind ourself concealed,
Should startle most;

Assassin, hid in our apartment,
Be horror's least.

The prudent carries a revolver,
He bolts the door,
O'erlooking a superior spectre
More near.

70

SHE died,—this was the way she died;
And when her breath was done,
Took up her simple wardrobe
And started for the sun.

Her little figure at the gate
The angels must have spied,
Since I could never find her
Upon the mortal side.

71

WAIT till the majesty of Death
Invests so mean a brow!
Almost a powdered footman
Might dare to touch it now!

Wait till in everlasting robes
This democrat is dressed,
Then prate about "preferment"
And "station" and the rest!

Around this quiet courtier
Obsequious angels wait!
Full royal is his retinue,
Full purple is his state!

A lord might dare to lift the hat
To such a modest clay,
Since that my Lord, "the Lord of lords"
Receives unblushingly!

72

WENT up a year this evening!
I recollect it well!
Amid no bells nor bravos
The bystanders will tell!
Cheerful, as to the village,
Tranquil, as to repose,
Chastened, as to the chapel,
This humble tourist rose.
Did not talk of returning,
Alluded to no time
When, were the gales propitious,
We might look for him;
Was grateful for the roses
In life's diverse bouquet,
Talked softly of new species
To pick another day.
Beguiling thus the wonder,
The wondrous nearer drew;
Hands bustled at the moorings—
The crowd respectful grew.

Ascended from our vision
To countenances new!
A difference, a daisy,
Is all the rest I knew!

73

TAKEN from men this morning,
Carried by men to-day,
Met by the gods with banners
Who marshalled her away.

One little maid from playmates,
One little mind from school,—
There must be guests in Eden;
All the rooms are full.

Far as the east from even,
Dim as the border star,—
Courtiers quaint, in kingdoms,
Our departed are.

74

WHAT inn is this
Where for the night
Peculiar traveller comes?
Who is the landlord?
Where the maids?
Behold, what curious rooms!
No ruddy fires on the hearth,
No brimming tankards flow.

Necromancer, landlord,
Who are these below?

75

It was not death, for I stood up,
And all the dead lie down;
It was not night, for all the bells
Put out their tongues, for noon.

It was not frost, for on my flesh
I felt siroccos crawl,—
Nor fire, for just my marble feet
Could keep a chancel cool.

And yet it tasted like them all;
The figures I have seen
Set orderly, for burial,
Reminded me of mine,

As if my life were shaven
And fitted to a frame,
And could not breathe without a key;
And 'twas like midnight, some,

When everything that ticked has stopped,
And space stares, all around,
Or grisly frosts, first autumn morns,
Repeal the beating ground.

But most like chaos,—stopless, cool,—
Without a chance or spar,

Or even a report of land
To justify despair.

76

I SHOULD not dare to leave my friend,
Because—because if he should die
While I was gone, and I—too late—
Should reach the heart that wanted me;

If I should disappoint the eyes
That hunted, hunted so, to see,
And could not bear to shut until
They "noticed" me—they noticed me;

If I should stab the patient faith
So sure I'd come—so sure I'd come,
It listening, listening, went to sleep
Telling my tardy name,—

My heart would wish it broke before,
Since breaking then, since breaking then,
Were useless as next morning's sun,
Where midnight frosts had lain!

77

*G*REAT streets of silence led away
To neighborhoods of pause;
Here was no notice, no dissent,
No universe, no laws.

By clocks 'twas morning, and for night
The bells at distance called;
But epoch had no basis here,
For period exhaled.

78

A THROE upon the features,
A hurry in the breath,
An ecstasy of parting
Denominated "Death,"—

An anguish at the mention,
Which, when to patience grown,
I've known permission given
To rejoin its own.

79

OF tribulation these are they
Denoted by the white;
The spangled gowns, a lesser rank
Of victors designate.

All these did conquer; but the ones
Who overcame most times
Wear nothing commoner than snow,
No ornament but palms.

Surrender is a sort unknown
On this superior soil;
Defeat, an outgrown anguish,
Remembered as the mile

[203]

Our panting ankle barely gained
When night devoured the road;
But we stood whispering in the house,
And all we said was "Saved!"

80

I THINK just how my shape will rise
When I shall be forgiven,
Till hair and eyes and timid head
Are out of sight, in heaven.

I think just how my lips will weigh
With shapeless, quivering prayer
That you, so late, consider me,
The sparrow of your care.

I mind me that of anguish sent,
Some drifts were moved away
Before my simple bosom broke,—
And why not this, if they?

And so, until delirious borne
I con that thing,—"forgiven,"—
Till with long fright and longer trust
I drop my heart, unshriven!

81

AFTER a hundred years
Nobody knows the place,—
Agony, that enacted there,
Motionless as peace.

[204]

Weeds triumphant ranged,
Strangers strolled and spelled
At the lone orthography
Of the elder dead.

Winds of summer fields
Recollect the way,—
Instinct picking up the key
Dropped by memory.

82

LAY this laurel on the one
Too intrinsic for renown.
Laurel! veil your deathless tree,—
Him you chasten, that is he!

83

THIS world is not conclusion;
    A sequel stands beyond,
Invisible, as music,
    But positive, as sound.
It beckons and it baffles;
    Philosophies don't know,
And through a riddle, at the last,
    Sagacity must go.
To guess it puzzles scholars;
    To gain it, men have shown
Contempt of generations,
    And crucifixion known.

[205]

*W*E learn in the retreating
 How vast an one
Was recently among us.
 A perished sun

Endears in the departure
 How doubly more
Than all the golden presence
 It was before!

*T*HEY say that "time assuages,"—
 Time never did assuage;
An actual suffering strengthens,
 As sinews do, with age.

Time is a test of trouble,
 But not a remedy.
If such it prove, it prove too
 There was no malady.

*W*E cover thee, sweet face.
 Not that we tire of thee,
But that thyself fatigue of us;
 Remember, as thou flee,
We follow thee until
 Thou notice us no more,
And then, reluctant, turn away

And kingdoms, like the orchard,
  Flit russetly away.

93

THE distance that the dead have gone
  Does not at first appear;
Their coming back seems possible
  For many an ardent year.

And then, that we have followed them
  We more than half suspect,
So intimate have we become
  With their dear retrospect.

94

How dare the robins sing,
  When men and women hear
Who since they went to their account
  Have settled with the year!—
Paid all that life had earned
  In one consummate bill,
And now, what life or death can do
  Is immaterial.
Insulting is the sun
  To him whose mortal light,
Beguiled of immortality,
  Bequeaths him to the night.
In deference to him
  Extinct be every hum,
Whose garden wrestles with the dew,
  At daybreak overcome!

95

DEATH is like the insect
    Menacing the tree,
Competent to kill it,
    But decoyed may be.

Bait it with the balsam,
    Seek it with the knife,
Baffle, if it cost you
    Everything in life.

Then, if it have burrowed
    Out of reach of skill,
Ring the tree and leave it,—
    'Tis the vermin's will.

'Tis sunrise, little maid, hast thou
    No station in the day?
'Twas not thy wont to hinder so,—
    Retrieve thine industry.

'Tis noon, my little maid, alas!
    And art thou sleeping yet?
The lily waiting to be wed,
    The bee, dost thou forget?

My little maid, 'tis night; alas,
    That night should be to thee
Instead of morning! Hadst thou broached
    Thy little plan to me,

Dissuade thee if I could not, sweet,
   I might have aided thee.

97

EACH that we lose takes part of us;
A crescent still abides,
Which like the moon, some turbid night,
Is summoned by the tides.

98

NOT any higher stands the grave
   For heroes than for men;
Not any nearer for the child
   Than numb three-score and ten.

This latest leisure equal lulls
   The beggar and his queen;
Propitiate this democrat
   A summer's afternoon.

99

As far from pity as complaint,
   As cool to speech as stone,
As numb to revelation
   As if my trade were bone.

As far from time as history,
   As near yourself to-day
As children to the rainbow's scarf,
   Or sunset's yellow play

To eyelids in the sepulchre.
    How still the dancer lies,
While color's revelations break,
    And blaze the butterflies!

100

'Tis whiter than an Indian pipe,
    'Tis dimmer than a lace;
No stature has it, like a fog,
    When you approach the place.

Not any voice denotes it here,
    Or intimates it there;
A spirit, how doth it accost?
    What customs hath the air?

This limitless hyperbole
    Each one of us shall be;
'Tis drama, if (hypothesis)
    It be not tragedy!

She laid her docile crescent down,
    And this confiding stone
Still states, to dates that have forgot,
    The news that she is gone.

So constant to its stolid trust,
    The shaft that never knew,
It shames the constancy that fled
    Before its emblem flew.

BLESS God, he went as soldiers,
    His musket on his breast;
Grant, God, he charge the bravest
    Of all the martial blest.

Please God, might I behold him
    In epauletted white,
I should not fear the foe then,
    I should not fear the fight.

IMMORTAL is an ample word
    When what we need is by,
But when it leaves us for a time,
    'Tis a necessity.

Of heaven above the firmest proof
    We fundamental know,
Except for its marauding hand,
    It had been heaven below.

WHERE every bird is bold to go,
    And bees abashless play,
The foreigner before he knocks
    Must thrust the tears away.

THE grave my little cottage is,
    Where, keeping house for thee,

I make my parlor orderly,
   And lay the marble tea,

For two divided, briefly,
   A cycle, it may be,
Till everlasting life unite
   In strong society.

106

THIS was in the white of the year,
   That was in the green,
Drifts were as difficult then to think
   As daisies now to be seen.

Looking back is best that is left,
   Or if it be before,
Retrospection is prospect's half,
   Sometimes almost more.

107

SWEET hours have perished here;
   This is a mighty room;
Within its precincts hopes have played,—
   Now shadows in the tomb.

108

ME! Come! My dazzled face
In such a shining place!

Me! Hear! My foreign ear
The sounds of welcome near!

The saints shall meet
Our bashful feet.

My holiday shall be
That they remember me;

My paradise, the fame
That they pronounce my name.

109

FROM us she wandered now a year,
    Her tarrying unknown;
If wilderness prevent her feet,
    Or that ethereal zone

No eye hath seen and lived,
    We ignorant must be.
We only know what time of year
    We took the mystery.

110

I WISH I knew that woman's name,
    So, when she comes this way,
To hold my life, and hold my ears,
    For fear I hear her say

She's "sorry I am dead," again,
    Just when the grave and I
Have sobbed ourselves almost to sleep,—
    Our only lullaby.

[2 1 5]

111

BEREAVED of all, I went abroad,
No less bereaved to be
Upon a new peninsula,—
The grave preceded me,

Obtained my lodgings ere myself,
And when I sought my bed,
The grave it was, reposed upon
The pillow for my head.

I waked, to find it first awake,
I rose,—it followed me;
I tried to drop it in the crowd,
To lose it in the sea,

In cups of artificial drowse
To sleep its shape away,—
The grave was finished, but the spade
Remained in memory.

112

I FELT a funeral in my brain,
And mourners, to and fro,
Kept treading, treading, till it seemed
That sense was breaking through.

And when they all were seated,
A service like a drum
Kept beating, beating, till I thought
My mind was going numb.

And then I heard them lift a box,
  And creak across my soul
With those same boots of lead, again.
  Then space began to toll

As all the heavens were a bell,
  And Being but an ear,
And I and silence some strange race,
  Wrecked, solitary, here.

113

I MEANT to find her when I came;
  Death had the same design;
But the success was his, it seems,
  And the discomfit mine.

I meant to tell her how I longed
  For just this single time;
But Death had told her so the first,
  And she had hearkened him.

To wander now is my abode;
  To rest,—to rest would be
A privilege of hurricane
  To memory and me.

114

I SING to use the waiting,
  My bonnet but to tie,
And shut the door unto my house;
  No more to do have I,

Till, his best step approaching,
    We journey to the day,
And tell each other how we sang
    To keep the dark away.

115

A sickness of this world it most occasions
    When best men die;
A wishfulness their far condition
    To occupy.

A chief indifference, as foreign
    A world must be
Themselves forsake contented,
    For Deity.

116

Superfluous were the sun
    When excellence is dead;
He were superfluous every day,
    For every day is said

That syllable whose faith
    Just saves it from despair,
And whose "I'll meet you" hesitates—
    If love inquire, "Where?"

Upon his dateless fame
    Our periods may lie,
As stars that drop anonymous
    From an abundant sky.

So proud she was to die
  It made us all ashamed
That what we cherished, so unknown
  To her desire seemed.

So satisfied to go
  Where none of us should be,
Immediately, that anguish stooped
  Almost to jealousy.

Tie the strings to my life, my Lord,
  Then I am ready to go!
Just a look at the horses—
  Rapid! That will do!

Put me on the firmest side,
  So I shall never fall;
For we must ride to the Judgment,
  And it's partly down hill.

But never I mind the bridges,
  And never I mind the sea;
Held fast in everlasting race
  By my own choice and thee.

Good-by to the life I used to live,
  And the world I used to know;
And kiss the hills for me, just once;
  Now I am ready to go!

THE dying need but little, dear,—
   A glass of water's all,
A flower's unobtrusive face
   To punctuate the wall,

A fan, perhaps, a friend's regret,
   And certainly that one
No color in the rainbow
   Perceives when you are gone.

THERE's something quieter than sleep
   Within this inner room!
It wears a sprig upon its breast,
   And will not tell its name.

Some touch it and some kiss it,
   Some chafe its idle hand;
It has a simple gravity
   I do not understand!

While simple-hearted neighbors
   Chat of the "early dead,"
We, prone to periphrasis,
   Remark that birds have fled!

121

THREE weeks passed since I had seen her,—
   Some disease had vexed;

'Twas with text and village singing
  I beheld her next,

And a company—our pleasure
  To discourse alone;
Gracious now to me as any,
  Gracious unto none.

Borne, without dissent of either,
  To the parish night;
Of the separated people
  Which are out of sight?

122

I breathed enough to learn the trick,
  And now, removed from air,
I simulate the breath so well,
  That one, to be quite sure

The lungs are stirless, must descend
  Among the cunning cells,
And touch the pantomime himself.
  How cool the bellows feels!

123

I wonder if the sepulchre
Is not a lonesome way,
When men and boys, and larks and June
Go down the fields to hay!

IF tolling bell I ask the cause,
  "A soul has gone to God,"
I'm answered in a lonesome tone;
  Is heaven then so sad?

That bells should joyful ring to tell
  A soul had gone to heaven,
Would seem to me the proper way
  A good news should be given.

IF I may have it when it's dead
  I will contented be;
If just as soon as breath is out
  It shall belong to me,

Until they lock it in the grave,
  'Tis bliss I cannot weigh,
For though they lock thee in the grave,
  Myself can hold the key.

Think of it, lover! I and thee
  Permitted face to face to be;
After a life, a death we'll say,—
  For death was that, and this is thee.

126

BEFORE the ice is in the pools,
  Before the skaters go,

Or any cheek at nightfall
   Is tarnished by the snow,

Before the fields have finished,
   Before the Christmas tree,
Wonder upon wonder
   Will arrive to me!

What we touch the hems of
   On a summer's day;
What is only walking
   Just a bridge away;

That which sings so, speaks so,
   When there's no one here,—
Will the frock I wept in
   Answer me to wear?

127

I HEARD a fly buzz when I died;
   The stillness round my form
Was like the stillness in the air
   Between the heaves of storm.

The eyes beside had wrung them dry,
   And breaths were gathering sure
For that last onset, when the king
   Be witnessed in his power.

I willed my keepsakes, signed away
   What portion of me I

Could make assignable,—and then
　　There interposed a fly,

With blue, uncertain, stumbling buzz,
　　Between the light and me;
And then the windows failed, and then
　　I could not see to see.

128

ADRIFT! A little boat adrift!
　　And night is coming down!
Will no one guide a little boat
　　Unto the nearest town?

So sailors say, on yesterday,
　　Just as the dusk was brown,
One little boat gave up its strife
　　And gurgled down and down.

But angels say, on yesterday,
　　Just as the dawn was red,
One little boat o'erspent with gales
Retrimmed its masts, redecked its sails
　　Exultant, onward sped!

129

THERE's been a death in the opposite house
　　As lately as to-day.
I know it by the numb look
　　Such houses have alway.

[2 2 4]

The neighbors rustle in and out,
   The doctor drives away.
A window opens like a pod,
   Abrupt, mechanically;

Somebody flings a mattress out,—
   The children hurry by;
They wonder if It died on that,—
   I used to when a boy.

The minister goes stiffly in
   As if the house were his,
And he owned all the mourners now,
   And little boys besides;

And then the milliner, and the man
   Of the appalling trade,
To take the measure of the house.
There'll be that dark parade

Of tassels and of coaches soon;
   It's easy as a sign,—
The intuition of the news
   In just a country town.

130

WE never know we go,—when we are going
   We jest and shut the door;
Fate following behind us bolts it,
   And we accost no more.

[2 2 5]

131

Iᴛ struck me every day
  The lightning was as new
As if the cloud that instant slit
  And let the fire through.

It burned me in the night,
  It blistered in my dream;
It sickened fresh upon my sight
  With every morning's beam.

I thought that storm was brief,—
  The maddest, quickest by;
But Nature lost the date of this,
  And left it in the sky.

Wᴀᴛᴇʀ is taught by thirst;
Land, by the oceans passed;
  Transport, by throe;
Peace, by its battles told;
Love, by memorial mould;
  Birds, by the snow.

Wᴇ thirst at first,—'tis Nature's act;
  And later, when we die,
A little water supplicate
  Of fingers going by.

It intimates the finer want,
    Whose adequate supply
Is that great water in the west
    Termed immortality.

134

A CLOCK stopped—not the mantel's;
    Geneva's farthest skill
Can't put the puppet bowing
    That just now dangled still.

An awe came on the trinket!
    The figures hunched with pain,
Then quivered out of decimals
    Into degreeless noon.

It will not stir for doctors,
    This pendulum of snow;
The shopman importunes it,
    While cool, concernless No

Nods from the gilded pointers,
    Nods from the seconds slim,
Decades of arrogance between
    The dial life and him.

135

*A*LL overgrown by cunning moss,
    All interspersed with weed,
The little cage of "Currer Bell,"*
    In quiet Haworth laid.

[227]

This bird, observing others,
    When frosts too sharp became,
Retire to other latitudes,
    Quietly did the same.

But differed in returning;
    Since Yorkshire hills are green,
Yet not in all the nests I meet
    Can nightingale be seen.

Gathered from any wanderings,
    Gethsemane can tell
Through what transporting anguish
    She reached the asphodel!

Soft fall the sounds of Eden
    Upon her puzzled ear;
Oh, what an afternoon for heaven,
    When Brontë entered there!

136

A TOAD can die of light!
    Death is the common right
Of toads and men,—
Of earl and midge

The privilege.
    Why swagger then?
The gnat's supremacy
Is large as thine.

$\mathcal{F}$ar from love the Heavenly Father
   Leads the chosen child;
Oftener through realm of briar
   Than the meadow mild,

Oftener by the claw of dragon
   Than the hand of friend,
Guides the little one predestined
   To the native land.

$\mathcal{A}$ LONG, long sleep, a famous sleep
   That makes no show for dawn
By stretch of limb or stir of lid,—
   An independent one.

Was ever idleness like this?
   Within a hut of stone
To bask the centuries away
   Nor once look up for noon?

'$\mathcal{T}$was just this time last year I died.
   I know I heard the corn,
When I was carried by the farms,—
   It had the tassels on.

I thought how yellow it would look
   When Richard went to mill;

And then I wanted to get out,
    But something held my will.

I thought just how red apples wedged
    The stubble's joints between;
And carts went stooping round the fields
    To take the pumpkins in.

I wondered which would miss me least,
    And when Thanksgiving came,
If father'd multiply the plates
    To make an even sum.

And if my stocking hung too high,
    Would it blur the Christmas glee,
That not a Santa Claus could reach
    The altitude of me?

But this sort grieved myself, and so
    I thought how it would be
When just this time, some perfect year,
    Themselves should come to me.

140

On this wondrous sea,
    Sailing silently,
Knowest thou the shore
    Ho! pilot, ho!
Where no breakers roar,
    Where the storm is o'er?

In the silent west
Many sails at rest,
    Their anchors fast;
Thither I pilot thee,—
Land, ho! Eternity!
    Ashore at last!

The Best of the World's Best Books
COMPLETE LIST OF TITLES IN
THE MODERN LIBRARY

For convenience in ordering use number at right of title

MISCELLANEOUS

MODERN LIBRARY GIANTS

A series of full-sized library editions of books that formerly were available only in cumbersome and expensive sets.
THE MODERN LIBRARY GIANTS REPRESENT A
SELECTION OF THE WORLD'S GREATEST BOOKS

These volumes contain from 600 to 1,400 pages each
